LEADERSHIFT

LEADERSHIFT

Reinventing leadership for the age of mass collaboration

Emmanuel Gobillot

KOGAN
PAGE

London and Philadelphia

First published in Great Britain and the United States in 2009 by Kogan Page Limited

120 Pentonville Road
London N1 9JN
United Kingdom
www.koganpage.com

525 South 4th Street, #241
Philadelphia PA 19147
USA

© Emmanuel Gobillot, 2009

ISBN   978 0 7494 5531 6

British Library Cataloguing-in-Publication Data

A CIP record for this book is available from the British Library.

Library of Congress Cataloging-in-Publication Data

Gobillot, Emmanuel.
   Leadershift : reinventing leadership for the age of mass collaboration / Emmanuel Gobillot.
       p. cm.
   Includes index.
   ISBN 978-0-7494-5531-6
   1. Leadership. I. Title.
   HM1261.G632 2009
   303.3'4–dc22

                              2009008502

Typeset by JS Typesetting Ltd, Porthcawl, Mid Glamorgan
Printed and bound in India by Replika Press Pvt Ltd

To Charlotte and George
for questioning everything I think, say or do,
even if I don't always come across as grateful when you're doing it!

Contents

Acknowledgements

From the day I got my first cassette tape as a child (Kate Bush's *The Kick Inside* if you must know) I discovered the fascinating world of acknowledgements. Here was a way of getting closer to the artist. Here I could not only enjoy the work itself but understand more about its creation and the person behind it. Later, as I became an avid reader as well as a music fan, my love for acknowledgements never disappeared. Until, that is, I realized how hard it was to write my own. There is something really difficult about naming everyone who contributed to your work when you have been influenced by so many people without, at times, even realizing it. So I want to start by apologizing to anyone I might have omitted from this. I did not do so willingly or knowingly.

Along with desk and library-based research, most of my ideas come from and are refined with executives in organizations I am lucky to visit and work alongside. There are some in particular who have given me license to operate freely within their businesses in a way that has directly enriched this text.

My thanks and gratitude go to Hayko Kroese, Global Head of Human Resources at Philips, and his team (especially Lucille Adriaens, Country Talent Manager Benelux, Kirsten Menes, Senior Director

Global Talent Management and Charlotte Ruminak, Regional Talent Management Philips Lighting APAC) for taking me around the world to meet some incredible people in an incredible organization.

The Unicredit Group leadership development centre (Unimanagement) in Turin, Italy, is one of the most exciting places I have had the experience of working in. The centre, designed from the ground up with learning in mind by Anna Simioni, CEO of Unimanagement and her team of talented development professionals, is a testament to how physical environments can influence learning. Anna herself, along with Davide Paganoni and David Landau, have been wonderful guides through my own thoughts, challenging me to excel at every step of the way.

My thanks also go to the good people at Carlsberg Group with whom I have had so much fun for the last five years all over the world. In particular I want to thank Majvi Wulff-Christensen, Group Vice President of Development, Lisbeth Sundby, Director of Talent and Dorota Cagiel, Human Resources Director (Poland), for giving me so many opportunities and so much support.

I also want to thank Evan Wittenberg and his team at Google University (in particular Rachel Kay and Alana Weiss from the School of Leadership Development) for trusting me enough to let me roam the corridors of Googleplex and meet some of the most talented and inquisitive people I have ever met.

Everyone I have had the chance to meet at Rabobank deserves credit for inspiring me to think more deeply about the role business plays in our lives and the responsibilities it must carry as a result. In particular I must thank Ivo Bilsen, Annemieke Bok, Henny Van Egmond, Rick Garrelf and Bert Mertens for their support and insights.

I would also like to thank Katherine Thomas for her support. Katherine not only improved the early drafts of this book, but, because of her role as Group Director of Talent and Leadership Development at BT plc, challenged me to make the ideas relevant to real executives with real jobs in the real economy rather than the conceptual executives and organizations that inhabit my consultant's and academic's head.

The craft of writing can be a long and lonely existence. I want to thank my publisher Helen Kogan and her team at Kogan Page. Special thanks go to Hannah Berry, whose project this was, for patiently listening to my poor excuses and adjusting her deadlines accordingly as well as for putting up with my strange ideas for generating titles, designing covers and my undying love of fonts (bordering, I admit, on psychosis).

You would not be holding this book if it wasn't for all the people who bought (thereby encouraging my publisher to have faith in me), read (thereby encouraging me to have faith in myself) and commented on (thereby encouraging me to challenge my own and my publisher's faith) *The Connected Leader*. It is because of you that I have been lucky enough to be given the chance to write another book. To the thousands of people who have listened and challenged my ideas as I travelled the world presenting *The Connected Leader* keynote, your words are somewhere in this new book and for that I thank you.

Finally, my usual disclaimer applies. Any omissions or mistakes are entirely mine; just thank these people that they have helped me keep them to a minimum.

Introduction

'As for the future, your task is not to foresee it, but to enable it.'

Antoine de Saint-Exupéry (1900–44)

'And if you throw enough snowballs you can even get banned.' Those were the words uttered, with just a bit too much enthusiasm for my liking, by my then six-year-old son, George, which were to lead me on the search that would eventually become this book. To be exact it was the ensuing discussion rather than the above statement that would do it.

George, or rather his avatar (an online representation of himself, in this case a blue penguin), was taking me on a visit to his igloo on Club Penguin when he made his snowball observation. An online community for children, Club Penguin has since been bought by Disney for US\$700 million. George and his sister Charlotte had been inhabitants of the snow-covered world for some time when I decided to take a closer look. At its simplest, Club Penguin can be described as an online world where children meet other children and play games. Playing games earns them coins, which they can redeem for items for their avatar out of the Club's ever-changing catalogue. Options include a new igloo, clothing, items to decorate their igloos and even pets (called puffles) for which they will have to buy food.

The discussion George and I were having was about the rules of the Club. 'How do you know what is right and wrong?' I had asked. George's explanation was that 'you tell Club Penguin when you think someone is doing something wrong and then they get banned' (there is no second chance according to George). 'You can't tell your real name or where you live or stuff like that because that's not right but the thing I don't get is why you can't just say sorry and not get banned.' This was what did it for me. Why, George was asking, is someone else making decisions about what is right when the world is supposed to belong to me?

Club Penguin is a MMORPG (massively multiplayer online role-playing game). MMORPGs are online games played in communities that resemble social networks. Other well-known MMORPGs are Second Life (SL) and World of Warcraft (WoW). The narrative in WoW is pretty much written by the company. It is a game. It has a goal. It is more flexible than many games as players aim to build coalitions and teams but Blizzard Entertainment Inc, owners of the World, have an underpinning narrative for the story, which as a player you will be called on to shape. At the other extreme stands SL, a place where avatars roam freely in a land they build. There, the narrative is entirely user-generated. Linden Lab (the company behind SL) have not created a story, rather they have built an infrastructure for you to create a world. Somewhere in the middle, Club Penguin has a semi-user-generated narrative, hence George's confusion – if you are the narrative writers, then shouldn't you also be writing the rules? (We will come back to avatars and the importance of narrative later.)

This discussion I was having with my son brought home to me (literally) what *Wikinomics* authors D Tapscott and A D Williams have called the perfect storm. In their seminal bestseller they argue, recalling the assertion made by the economist Joseph Schumpeter, that 'gales of creative destruction' lead to development and that 'when technology, demographics and global economics collide you are faced with a category 6 business revolution'. When six-year-old

George uses online communities to create a story with the next-door neighbour and with a little boy in India[1], advising you in the process to be wary of US servers past two o'clock UK time as 'they become slow because American kids check out their puffles', you know something is afoot in the way we live. It is not only because there is something exciting about a six-year-old being conversant with time differences or getting the concept of server capacity that we can see that indeed, Tapscott and Williams make an irrefutable claim – mass participation *does* change everything.

So what of my quest? Why did this conversation with George start me on another book?

As parents we get very few tips on how to raise our children. We may, if we are that way inclined, buy a few books. In the main though, we get our clues from the way we were raised. As children we developed within a given environment. Our experiences shaped our lives. So when the experiences of your children are fundamentally different from the experiences you had as a child, you realize that looking to your own childhood to guide effective upbringing may no longer be the best source of insight. Had I been a child psychologist you could well have been holding a book called *How to bring up George*. But I am not a child psychologist. So the discussion with George took me to another place and another question.

If mass collaboration changes everything, how does it change the way we lead?[2]

Millions of people with experiences similar to George's are already entering the workplace. The so-called millennials are in your building as we speak, expecting to craft the narrative and the rules of your business. What does it mean for the way we lead? A band of coders writes a piece of software in their spare time that captures real market share over real established businesses. What does that mean for the role of the leader?

And it's not just in the virtual or software world that things are changing. Even in some of the most expert fields of human endeavour the rules are changing. Amateurs sitting in front of their home computers are helping NASA solve problems previously tackled by armies of PhDs (and they're making a good job of it). What does that mean for the way we build organizations?

We will come back to these examples and a multitude of others as our story unfolds but what we will find is that there are two themes. It is these two themes that have come to underpin my research.

First, George is not the only one experiencing 'the creation confusion'. Mass collaboration in our current world is expressing itself through the discomfort of its participants, who have been offered a role in the narrative but are being kept away from creating the rules. To become fully optimal (and arguably commercially viable), mass collaboration requires a form of leadership that is prepared to let go of the experience, expertise and control it holds precious.

Second, given that there are few, if any, clues from the past to inform the way we can be successful in the future, we are unlikely to get insights into becoming leaders in the next generation by looking back at our experiences or our elders.

But if the quote by Antoine de Saint-Exupéry that opens this introduction is right (and no French citizen would ever suggest otherwise), our role is not to guess what happens next or try to foresee the future. Our role as leaders is to decide what we want this future to be. Our role is to view our organizations through the lens of 48 million avatars currently roaming the web[3], 10 per cent of whom do so for more than 10 hours a day. Our role is to decide how we can capture the energy of mass collaboration to redefine first our business models and ultimately the very meaning of business.

If your aspirations are different as you struggle to grow your business under ever more challenging economic conditions I don't blame you. So let me set out a shorter-range goal. Our role is to understand how we fast-forward to the future because, right here, right now, unless we understand the new rules of leadership, we are sub-optimizing our businesses.

My only hypothesis as I embarked on my search was that leadership in a world underpinned by mass participation might need to change. Wanting to apply some rigour to my investigation I was even prepared to accept that nothing would change. Slowly, as I meandered through the unfamiliar territories of the virtual organization and social networks I began to shape a new hypothesis.

The social, collaborative and virtual networking phenomena have far deeper implications than just changing the way we do business. They are changing business itself. Business is no longer hierarchical (as it still remains in the main today) nor is it personal (as we were keen to suggest in the 1990s). Mass participation makes business social. Mass collaboration makes it communal. This is changing the nature of roles. Whilst sought and welcomed, leadership in communities is intrinsically linked to narrative, task and contribution rather than power, role and accountability. Therefore, by understanding the communal landscape we can understand the nature of the leadership requirements and start to develop new models of leadership effectiveness.

As I set out to research my hypothesis, the new leadership proposition this book makes evolved. Because communities are always evolving, the rules of engagement are constantly changing but what remains true is a certain philosophy of leading, which I hope to convey here. No longer in charge of setting a direction, the role of the leader is to help the community find its voice. From there their communities will find their own direction and narrative as they set out to succeed.

Most of what we do as leaders is engineering. We try to engineer behaviours in others through engineering more effective and humane hierarchies. We use our influencing tactics to get customers to buy and employees to perform. Faced with 'the influencers' made famous by Malcolm Gladwell's *The Tipping Point,* we endeavour to segment our customer base to identify who really matters and thereby engineer attraction, share of wallet extension and retention strategies. Faced with a talent shortage we segment our employee base to identify who really performs and devise attraction, performance and retention strategies. Faced with any narrative our leadership answer is always the same – find, attract, nurture and convince by engineering solutions to problems. Mass collaboration requires that we find a new modus operandi.

Our leadership models have been influenced by our understanding of the psychology of both leaders and followers. We look for deficits that need to be fixed rather than strengths that can be augmented. We focus on why individuals do what they do, hoping that by deepening our understanding we can engineer better control mechanisms.

Leading in mass participation requires us to don our Indiana Jones hats and become social anthropologists, focusing on the communities that are created, rather than the psychology of any one individual who contributes to one or more of them. Mass collaboration is indeed a herd phenomenon where focusing on the masses pays off.

The aim of leadership will always be to secure engagement, alignment, accountability and commitment. What is changing is the way in which we will achieve these. If you ever feel that the world of leadership is getting tougher it is because it is. The reason this is being felt like never before is that the world opening in front of us is making many of our tried and tested success recipes redundant.

It would be disingenuous of me to suggest that I have all the answers and this book contains all the tools and the magic bullets you will need to succeed. Rather this book sets out a new leadership landscape and some new pictures of what success looks like.

Having read over 100 books, from the more classic leadership titles to the more adventurous anthropological searches of virtual worlds, consulted over 1,000 blog entries, spoken to over 200 executives from global corporations to local start-ups across Asia, Europe and the United States, the answer to my question 'If mass collaboration is a reality must the way we lead change?' met with a resounding yes. As our context is changing, in a way we can no longer stop, it won't change us, just make us irrelevant, unless we know how to act in this new paradigm.

The two questions publishers always ask when considering a new book proposal are 'Who is the audience?' and 'Why should they buy/read the book?'. My answer to these two questions is as follows.

The audience is anyone looking to make their organization more effective (be they private, public or not for profit). I hope to demonstrate that a new way to lead is neither an option nor some far-flung scenario but a current reality, the absence of which accounts for most of the challenges we face today, whilst its presence helps understand the success that some leaders experience.

The way I have organized the book should help you navigate the story. Ultimately I have tried to make it easy for you to write your own narrative. When my first book, *The Connected Leader,* was published, many reviews focused not so much on the content but rather on the way the book was organized. As this formula seemed to work I have tried to emulate it here. So, whilst the book is organized in chapters, pretty much as you would expect, I have also included a couple of devices that I hope will save you time.

First, let me walk you through the chapters. Chapters 1 to 5 paint a picture of the trends that are shaping a new business landscape. Chapter 1 looks at the nature of turbulence (both short term and long term) whilst Chapters 2 to 5 describe each of the trends that are shaping mass collaboration. Chapter 6 looks at the communities that emerge from mass collaboration and what lies at the root of their engagement. Equipped with an understanding of the opportunities offered by mass participation, Chapter 7 looks at what must change in the way we lead and what can stay the same.

Having looked at the 'why' and the 'what', Chapters 8, 9, 10 and 11 turn to the 'how' by looking at how leaders can fulfill their role (ie engaging, aligning, making accountable and ensuring commitment) in the age of mass collaboration. Each chapter looks at how we currently meet the challenge, why it is ineffective and how leaders will need to shift their mindset towards new priorities in the way they lead.

Finally Chapter 12 focuses on how we can get from where we are today to where we need to be tomorrow. But please don't rush to this last chapter all at once because chances are that unless you know something about what happens in the middle of the book, what comes at the end makes little sense.

One of the devices I used in my first book that appealed to reviewers was 'The 30 second recap', which I have decided to keep here. 'The 30 second recap' is a box you will find at the end of each chapter designed to summarize the ideas contained in that chapter. By reading this you will get the ideas of the book and more importantly you will be able to pass them on. You won't know where the idea came from, have data to support it or a couple of interesting stories to back it all up but you might not need that. What these recaps also help you do is decide whether you need to read the chapter. Maybe the chapter goes over territory you are familiar with or quite frankly it just doesn't interest you. Hopefully that way you may still want to read other parts and you won't get lost. As the book is about a new way to lead, the recap might not give you sufficient detail to put the idea into practice but at least you may want to use these to see which ideas you want to dig into and try out.

One new device I have introduced here is the 'Don't take my word for it' section. The idea is that you may want to find out more about my claims. You may feel that my word alone is not sufficient to convince you (making you incredibly similar to my children if you don't mind me sayings). If that's the case, at the end of the book, I have listed titles which will help you explore the ideas contained in the book in more depth. This isn't a full bibliography but, hopefully, a helpful source of interesting material.

So, yes you can read the book as a book. That's how it was written. But you can also use it as a toolkit if you wish.

Finally, I fondly remember my university days. Yet I also remember the panic induced by the last-minute cramming before the exam and the relief brought by the industrious people at Coles and Cliff and their magic notes. For the studious amongst you, Coles Notes are little books summarizing books on a variety of subjects, enabling you to get the idea without having to read the book.

Of course there will be no exam at the end of this book but the likelihood is that your schedule is similar to the five minutes available to anyone before going into an exam. So whilst I have included 'The

30 second recap' at the end of each chapter, I have decided to make things even easier for the 90 per cent of you (if statistics are to be believed) who are unlikely to make it past this introduction.

Below is what is effectively 'The four minute recap' (but I call it 'The cheat sheet' just to induce a slight feeling of guilt). For those of you standing in the bookshop and wondering why you should buy the book given that you can just read the cheat sheet and get the idea, I make you a promise – I have some amazing stories in here! For those of you ready to read the book, come and check out the T-shirt in Chapter 1.

The cheat sheet

There are four major societal trends that are forever transforming the way we live. As they continue to grow exponentially we face a stark choice – change the way we lead or become irrelevant.

The demographic trend means that we have multiple generations working alongside each other – each with demands and experiences that the others cannot comprehend. The expertise trend means that expertise is now to be found as much outside as inside the organization. The attention trend means that organizations have to fight harder than ever to capture the attention of employees and customers as information and interaction sources lay claim to limited time. Finally, the democratic trend means that the likelihood of leaders having direct control (rather than dotted lines or no lines at all) over their resources is remote.

Together these four trends spell (literally if you take their initials – DEAD) the death of leadership as we know it.

Mass participation communities are held together by an intricate and fluid process of relationships between members adopting different roles and involving themselves differently rather than a rigid organizational hierarchy. Whilst a leader's role has always been and will remain the creation of engagement, alignment, accountability and commitment to the organizational cause, in this new landscape the tools they use will need to change. Where once they relied on clarity, plans, roles and money to achieve these aims, they will need to find new tools.

Clarity is no longer feasible as a source of engagement. It is either impossible to provide or requires a one-sided view of the world (the leader's) to be constructed. This will not do for social engagement.

Simplicity, on the other hand, by providing simplification (ie simpler ways of operating) and coherence (ie a purpose for the effort) will play the role clarity once had.

Plans are only worth drafting if they are likely to be followed. When conversations are constantly helping the community to make sense of its environment, plans play no part in helping alignment. It is a narrative that provides the common language and story that ensures a community is aligned.

By defining accountabilities, roles are limiting to a certain set of circumstances. In an ever-changing environment, success is defined by having a community that is able to do whatever it takes to achieve an outcome, irrespective of whether an individual has been given a specific role or not. Our focus needs to change from roles to tasks that need to be fulfilled for the narrative to stay alive.

Finally, whilst money might secure involvement it will never secure commitment. It is contributing to the community and helping it grow (ie love) that keeps people committed to the efforts of the community. Understanding what people love and helping them find an outlet for that love is what will make leaders successful.

These dimensions are all critical. If you are missing one element you will not be successful (eg however strong your narrative, if no one loves it you will not create engagement). However, they do not have to be present to the same degree (eg a strong narrative can compensate for a weak task).

The role of the leader is to foster an environment where the conditions are right to attract a thriving community. It is not to create transactional involvement, as our leadership instinct too often leads us to do, by single-handedly creating or controlling the elements. Rather, leaders must shift their emphasis to the fostering of social engagement by valuing conversations that they otherwise might have deemed wasteful and inefficient. To be worth following, leaders will need to work primarily on the contribution they make, rather than the direction they give, to the community. This requires them to develop enough executive maturity (ie being comfortable in their own skin) to be able to see mass participation as an opportunity to create value rather than a threat to their existence.

Notes

1   To be fair George doesn't know if the penguin is actually from India or indeed if it is a boy or a girl, as this information was not exchanged

(that's purely his take on the situation). However, with 100 employees monitoring the site for safety and software filtering data for security, we can at least be pretty certain the little Indian penguin is actually a child!

2   Whilst I do recognize that the terms mass participation and mass collaboration convey different meaning (mass collaboration being a two-way process rather than the one-way effort participation suggests), to avoid repetition I will use them interchangeably throughout this book to describe communal efforts.

3   Data courtesy of Phil White of mmogdata.voig.com. Please note that the data change all the time as, much like our own, the online universe has been known to expand and contract but even with these changes the vastness of space remains.

1 The day of reckoning

'This was supposed to be the future so where is my jet pack?' As I saw this line emblazoned on a T-shirt I could not help but laugh aloud. I was laughing at myself as much as at the humorous line. Reading it brought back long-forgotten speculations from my childhood. As Proust so richly describes in *A la Recherche du Temps Perdu*,[1] when the taste of a simple cake takes him back to times past, I remembered the essays written on what life would be like after the year 2000. I remembered the excitement brought on by drawing little stick people with booster engines on their backs flying through the air as they went back home after a hard day's work. I was convinced that the food pills would taste delicious on my travels to the Moon. I couldn't wait to experience anti-gravity-hydrogen-powered-space-cars masterfully driven by robots. But as the T-shirt made clear and to recall the old adage, there is only one thing that can be predicted with any degree of accuracy and that is that any prediction you make is likely to turn out to be wrong.

A cynical reader might well argue that all authors of business books proclaim that the world is changing in radical ways and that only the books they have written will help you deal with the forthcoming paradigm shift (non-paradigm shifts seldom get written about). If you want to push the cynicism further you might well highlight that most predictions tend to be far enough away to ensure that should the future not unfold as predicted, no one will remember the prediction. On the other hand, they are typically close enough to warrant action on the part of the reader (after all, who cares about what will happen 10 or 15 years hence when tenure in a role averages 5 years?). The problem for me is that in this chapter I want to make the case that, unless leaders fundamentally change, they will become irrelevant. So picking a day of reckoning some four or five years away would imply that I am playing right into the cynics' hands. Therefore, rather than somehow try to disprove the cynics' claim, which I know to be true (I too err on the side of cynicism when I read), let me just start by laying down my cards.

The day Lehman Brothers fell might be the closest we will get to a day of reckoning. This type of turbulence is real, shocking and disturbs our leadership routines. It demands to be dealt with. For many it is a call to rethink the way our system works. It is a time for followers to hold leaders accountable and for leaders to question their modus operandi. The strength of the turbulence might even force us to question the effectiveness and nature of our tools (incentive schemes spring to mind). There are some clear demands which are made of leaders in these turbulent times.

First it is our role to bring reassurance. Don't get me wrong, reassurance does not require offering a solution. All are aware that answers are hard to come by and most understand that the systemic nature of the problems we face will require coordinated, global solutions that will not come from one leader alone. The fact is that any effort made to deliver an easy answer, especially by a leader seen to have created the mess in the first place, is more likely to create resentment than to reassure anyone. What I mean by reassurance is the need to know that our leaders understand the situation we are in. Followers want to see accountability and honesty in the people who lead.

When the CEOs of the big three motor companies take private jets to go to Washington to ask for economic help it is not only poor taste, but fundamentally reinforces the feeling that leaders are out of touch and do not understand the needs of their followers. On the other hand when one of the CEOs of the major banks says repeatedly 'I apologize for not having anticipated some of the issues we now face', he does more than show humility (or demand forgiveness in an effort to keep his job as cynics might claim), he provides reassurance by acknowledging what many feel.

Short-term turbulence requires leaders to work to reestablish their legitimacy through transparency, humility and commitment to their followers. This alone will provide followers with the reassurance they need that it is worth investing their efforts in following a leader. But reassurance alone does little to alleviate fears or take us forward to a solution. Our second task is to reestablish a sense of meaning in the economic activity.

In these testing times, many will question the very essence of what they are called to do. Is it all over for capitalism? Doesn't this prove once and for all that our system is faulty? Isn't the truth that our organizations are built on greed and exploitation? However logical or testing we think these questions might be, for followers to ask them is legitimate. Our role as leaders is not to shy away from those questions but to offer a forum for discussion. By forcing our organizations to rethink their very essence they will become stronger. Of course it is easier said (or written) than done. It requires courage on the part of leaders.

But our ability to rebuild confidence in our organizations and their leaders rests in our willingness to reconstruct a shared sense of meaning. The kind of economic circumstances we now face have a fundamental impact on our confidence. Where is this all going to end? Have we seen the worst or is this still to come? Why should I continue to be an economic agent (ie consume or produce) when there is so little certainty about what will happen next? This is where we need to shape answers to our problems. It is easier for meaning to be shared when it is co-created.

Meaning resides in our sense of purpose. The question we need to ask of our organizations and our followers is 'what is it that we can do together that cannot better be done by someone else?'. This question alone forces us to reengage in an economic debate. It takes us closer to the answer.

However all this is also dependent on our sense of community. When times are tough and incoherent we tend to retrench behind the boundaries we know and feel comfortable with. Employees become either compliant ('I will do what you say because I do not want to lose my job') or belligerent ('why should I trust anything you say when you say you value me but will sack me at the first opportunity') or downright combative ('I will make sure I am OK even if it is to the detriment of my colleagues').

Individuals fall back on themselves, potentially becoming self-serving, whilst organizations close their boundaries and countries their borders. We do not need to have read *1984* to know that any community pulls together when faced with a common enemy. All of these reactions are understandable and even, given our shared human history, legitimate. They are however highly destructive when it comes to building a strong organizational response.

For this reason alone we need to rebuild a sense of community that is as strong as the purpose we seek to fulfill. To do so, our strongest tool is our ability to hold courageous conversations. It is these that will build shared ownership in our future. We can do little on our own when it comes to building a community. Indeed we are dangerously mistaken if we think we can. There are however many potentially powerful communities in our organizations that tend to be sub-optimized when we operate in calmer times.

In my first book I wrote about the pockets of energy that are latent in all organizations. What I called 'the real organization', made up of the social networks that provide most of the energy to support our efforts, becomes even more critical in turbulent times. By understanding these networks and connecting to them leaders will be able to build the necessary bridge between these networks and the purpose the organization seeks to fulfill.

Yet, whilst this 'morning after the night before' type of turbulence questions the effectiveness of some leaders, it does not, in and of itself question the need for leadership. My argument here is that if you think we live in turbulent times you're in for a shock. There is a deeper kind of turbulence. There is a more pervasive kind of turbulence – one that is not as obvious and, as a result, to which we often fail to pay attention. This kind of turbulence does not express itself through a day of reckoning.

Think about it this way. For all intents and purposes, when you look in the mirror to compare yourself in the morning with how you looked the previous evening, bar the possible distortions brought about by a long day's work or a short night's sleep, your face looks broadly the same. We may well wake up one morning to find a world dramatically different from the one we left behind the evening before but it is still our world. Each day looks, and will continue to look, pretty much like the one before. The sun will come up and go down. But if we continue with this analogy we have to address one critical question. Do you look different today from how you did four or five years ago? Here, unfortunately, the difference is a lot plainer to see.

Even more prescient is the issue of whether this means you actually *think* that you look different. Many of us have attended school reunions only to be surprised at how badly time has affected others whilst leaving us unchanged. We are amazed at the way nature has been so unkind to others' hair and waistlines whilst it has been so kind to ours. We don't need quantum physics to know that change is relative to our own perspective.

My argument is that there is little value in leaders trying to get better at what they do, since what they do will become increasingly irrelevant given fundamental trends that are challenging the way we do business over and above the immediate turbulence we feel. The key to leaders' success is not their willingness to accept a day of reckoning and the efforts they make to prepare for this. Rather, it is their ability to embrace the idea that, given some fundamental trends, each day is a day of reckoning. This is the difference between surviving another day and creating the future. This is the difference between mediocrity and excellence. The good news is that most of the tools that will help us meet the challenge of these trends are also the ones that will help us get over the immediate challenges we face.

Research conducted by Dr Edward Miller, Dean of the Medical School and CEO Johns Hopkins University Hospital, suggests that within two years of coronary artery bypass grafting, 90 per cent of people have not changed their lifestyles despite the risks to their lives. Put another way, when faced with the choice change or die, 90 per cent of people seemingly chose death. On the basis that none of these trends threatens our actual survival, it is hard to see what kind of argument anyone could make to encourage change in the way we lead. Indeed, mass collaboration does not reject leadership.

The communities I describe in this book are crying out for leaders. Every challenge we face is met with a call for leadership. We have a thirst for people who can meet the only test of leadership – make us feel stronger and more capable. Our value and, ultimately, our survival as leaders, resides in our ability to meet the challenges dictated by four fundamental trends that make up mass collaboration. The real difficulty will be our ability to shift our emphasis when some of the things around us remain the same. The real challenge of mass collaboration is that it is practised with tools that do not necessarily facilitate it.

I do have, however, a belief that engaging in conversations that will help leaders paint a viscerally desired picture of the future is the way we will get over our reluctance to change. Of course, it will be a challenge to adjust our behaviour when most of the structures and systems we operate under reinforce the status quo. But it is a challenge we must face, for if we don't, taken together, these trends spell the potential death of leadership – literally.

- the demographic trend, which will make your experience irrelevant

Multiple generations, with multiple socio-cultural backgrounds, are now working alongside each other. Each brings with it its own hopes, fears, expectations and experiences, which the others don't understand and cannot relate to.

- the expertise trend, which will make your knowledge irrelevant

The expertise that drives organizational value increasingly resides in a network of relationships outside the managerial reach of the organization.

- the attention trend, which will make your efforts irrelevant

A collection of social and informational networks are coming to replace organizations as a source of coherence and cohesion for stakeholders.

- the democratic trend, which will make your power irrelevant

Consultants, interims, dotted line reports, part-time employees, casual labour and networks of associates have acquired an equal voice at the organizational table, outside a leader's span of control.

These shifts cannot be stopped. But they are not to be feared as they offer leaders new, efficient and effective sources of value generation. Let's take each in turn.

The 30 second recap

There are two kinds of turbulence that we face as leaders.

One type is short term – obvious, highly destructive and broadly felt. This is the type of turbulence that has been front of mind for most leaders recently as they have attempted to deal with the consequences of the sudden collapse of our financial system and the economic downturn this engendered.

Yet, there is also a more pervasive type of turbulence. Call it clear air turbulence if you will as it is seldom seen. As each day passes, the way leaders create value becomes less effective. The levers they rely on (experience, knowledge, effort and power) are being eroded by four major trends I will call the Demographic, Expertise, Attention and Democratic trends in the following chapters.

Whilst the first type of turbulence questions our effectiveness as leaders, the second kind questions the very essence of leadership.

Note

1   M Proust (1988) *A la Recherche du Temps Perdu, tome 1: Du Côté de chez Swann*, Gallimard.

2 The demographic trend

When two talented people had the idea of facilitating access to the whole of human knowledge it is unlikely they realized they were creating one of the world's most amazing businesses. It wasn't long after they set out to develop their business that the simplified design they adopted for their product (so different from the ones used by their competitors), their ubiquitous presence (making knowledge accessible quickly) and their relentless focus (doing one thing only and doing it well) would encourage many to spread the word and make theirs a product of choice for all. As their competitors struggled to grow profitably, their business was backed from day one.

The year was 1935. The two talented people were Allen Lane and V K Krishna Menon. This most amazing business was the British publisher, Penguin Books. Lane's idea was to democratize access to literature by providing quality books at the same price and locations as a pack of cigarettes. When many thought that the cheap selling price and the paperback format (so far reserved for second-rate novels) would lead anyone to bankruptcy, Lane and Menon knew that they could succeed. They rightly banked that a focus on design (a very clean cover to differentiate their offering from all other sub-standard works then offered in paperback), location (achieving presence in the places most likely to attract their target market) and seed funding gained from the purchase of 63,000 books by Woolworths would make the project worth it. They were right. Only 10 months after the company's launch on 30 July 1935, one million Penguin books had been printed.

The story of Penguin mirrors the story of that other democratizer of knowledge that arrived on the business scene some 60 years later – Google. In January 1996, like Lane, Larry Page was working on a project. Like Lane, he would soon be joined by a business partner (in his case, Sergey Brin). As it was with Penguin, the two Stanford University PhD students believed they could provide a better product than any competitor by relying on simplified design (to make the search results page faster), ubiquitous presence (using links as drivers of search results) and funding from one investor (US$100,000 from Andy Bechtolsheim, co-founder of Sun Microsystems). From Gutenberg to Google, the distribution of knowledge has always been a prime human concern.

As well as parallel histories, what Penguin and Google show is that any business idea is shaped by one critical force – the need to harness talent to optimize transaction costs by leveraging knowledge through the ambient technology of the time. But why does any of this matter?

To understand this we need to get back to my children, Charlotte and George, who, when aged nine and six respectively, without parental knowledge or consent, held a meeting to discuss the future of their education. Their conclusion was stark and called for no compromise: 'We've decided that we don't need to go to school any more because if we want to know anything we can just Google it up'. This has profound implications beyond my children's future development. Embedded into their forceful assertion are the two elements that make up the demographic trend.

The first element is the never-ending war for talent and, in particular, a new front opening in that war – the battle for leaders. By 2015 the working population of 'advanced' economies will have shrunk by 65 million.[1] In Europe, North America and Asia–Pacific the working age population is in steep decline, as much as –12 per cent in Japan[2] for example. In Europe, by the middle of this century, a third of the population will be retired[3] and by 2010 the United States will have 10 million vacancies.[4]

When you start digging in the numbers you realize that for these economies the picture is even more frightening when it comes to driving tomorrow's growth. Whilst it is unlikely that the demand for leaders will decline, it is certain that a healthy supply pipeline is necessary if you consider that 50 to 75 per cent of senior managers will be eligible for retirement by 2010.[5] Replacing them is critical. It will require a fundamental rethink of leadership development on a par with post-First and Second World War experiences. Fighting that battle will be hard when you also factor in the changing nature of both the job market and of the other people fighting the battle.

Even assuming that the US figure of 80 per cent of 'boomers' expecting to work past age 65 is replicated across the globe, you are still looking at a generational spread in organizations that is unprecedented.[6] This brings us to the second of the two elements that make up the demographic trend – the clash of experience.

The fact is that whilst some are facing leadership supply issues, others are not. If Pink Floyd are to be believed, 'another brick in the wall' doesn't sound like a good thing. In demographics, like with many other things, the BRIC countries (Brazil, Russia, India and China) are building a wall of success that will keep many other economies out. The working population of China is big enough to take every single US job and still have spare capacity. If you think that labour surplus is unqualified then think again. The number of those with upper quartile IQs in China is equivalent to the total North American population. As they come to realize the implications of the battle for leaders, policy makers will open up their frontiers to outside talent. Some 1 in 10 people living in the 'developed' world are already immigrants and that trend will more than likely continue. The implications are deep.

Think about it this way. What we learn shapes our experience, which in turn informs the way we lead. Leaders are the products of their pasts.

Their behaviour and, as a result, the type of leadership they offer is a combination of who they are as people and the situation they find themselves in. As geographical and socio-cultural differences enter the workplace at an unprecedented rate to fill the leadership gap, fewer people will be able to relate to their leaders' demands. This difference of experience, when viewed through an organizational lens, quickly becomes a clash of experience. No longer can leaders' experience help them comprehend others, and nor can others' experience help them understand the leadership leaders seek to provide. As this trend continues a leader's experience runs the risk of becoming irrelevant, if not altogether counterproductive. This problem is compounded by the fact that along with socio-cultural differences, we are also experiencing generational trends in organizations.

Over the last few decades, spurred on by marketing professionals in search of new revenue streams, the language of generations has been incorporated into the organization dictionary. Since then the business world has been full of 'Gen pick-your-letter'. A succession of writers, each hoping to 'own the space', has called the emerging generation something different and has used a somewhat different time bracket to define it. It has been called GenY, the Millennials or NetGet amongst other things and has been defined as starting as early as the early 1970s or as late as 1985. Most agree that it does not extend past the year 2000, I assume for the sake of neatness rather than science. If a generation is a group of people sharing common cultural references, one would have to argue that this is a somewhat long range to use to define one generation, and an even longer one to use in a study meant to generate meaningful insights. It is probably for that reason that the scrum to be recognized as the authority on the new generation has also led writers and journalists to make ever more extreme and exuberant claims about Generation Y (a term I use purely as it is the most commonly used). Given that many of these claims are not based on any research that would pass the test of science, the conclusions that may be drawn from them are erroneous at best.

Most researchers tend to compare themselves and their peers to the new generation. On that basis they outline stark differences. How often have you heard that the new generation is lazy compared with employees from an earlier generation, somehow feeling they are entitled to benefits without having to work for them? They are more individualistic than any previous generations. They demand too much and pay little respect to others and to hierarchies. Most of these assertions are, however, more likely to be indications of us getting old than a result of generational differences.

Take yourself back to your own youth. When you were in your early 20s didn't you want more? Didn't you always think there was a better way to do something than by obeying an arbitrary hierarchy? Didn't you want a better life than the one you thought your parents had? By comparing today's younger and older employees we are as likely to surface the nature of maturity as fundamental generational differences.

The fact that I get tired more quickly than my children when I play with them is more an indication of my age and deteriorating physical abilities than it is a clue as to some new generational stamina. To compare one generation with the next with any degree of certainty we must find a way of studying each generation using the same methods at the same time (ie inflict a test of some kind at the same age to students in the 1950s, 60s, 70s, 80s etc). This poses serious issues for today's researchers as most of the questions we would like answered today are to solve issues that no one paid much interest to in previous decades. That is until Jean M Twenge came along.

A Master's and later PhD student, plus a member herself of what she called 'Generation Me',[7] Jean was fascinated by generational differences, and also by the lack of any scientific research on the topic. As an academic she was also familiar with the rigour necessary to prove a point and less than overwhelmed by the evidence used to substantiate the claims made about a generation she herself represented. Thirteen years after she first started to research generational differences she published *Generation Me*, which to date has to be the most thorough exploration of the Generation Y phenomenon. Jean's research is critical on two accounts.

First, by using the now well-established psychological trait instruments (measuring recurring patterns of behaviours) she has finally brought some method to the assessment (ie really looking at behavioural

differences rather than anything else). But, and perhaps more fundamentally, by using these established psychological tools she also had
access to a huge cross-generational database, making a longitudinal
study possible. In fact, Jean M Twenge had enough data to look at the
behaviours of students of the same age throughout the 1950s, 60s, 70s,
80s and 90s. Armed with enough data points to make a pointillist pale
with envy, Jean exposed the real differences between generations.

This new generation, brought up with an idea of entitlement and an
unrealistic sense of possibilities,[8] is less likely to accept your leadership
than any generation in the past. Having discovered that their dreams
are unlikely to become reality members of this generation are also
more depressed and unfulfilled than their older siblings. Imagine a
workplace where you have up to three generations from numerous
continents with multiple socio-cultural backgrounds working alongside
each other. This demographic trend means that leaders will no longer
be able to rely on their experience to lead. But things get even worse
when you realize that along with their experience, their knowledge is
also in danger of becoming irrelevant.

If the demographic trend got you thinking, the expertise trend should
get you worried.

The 30 second recap

The first trend eroding the levers leaders rely on to create value is the
demographic trend.

In a nutshell, we now find ourselves with multiple generations with
multiple socio-cultural backgrounds working alongside each other. Each
brings with it its own hopes, fears, expectations and experiences that
other generations do not understand and to which they cannot relate.

As leaders we rely on our experiences to shape our leadership styles.
The way we lead is the outcome of who we are and the situations in which
we find ourselves. Yet, when that experience bears no resemblance to
the experience of people who we are called to lead, or in no way offers
us any insights into what might make us successful, we risk becoming
irrelevant.

Notes

1   New Zealand Department of Labour (2002).
2   Towers Perrin (2006) Talent management in the 21st Century, *World at Work Journal*, Q1.
3   Chartered Institute of Personnel and Development (2003).
4   *HR Magazine* (2003).
5   Forrester Research.
6   *Workforce* (2000) July.
7   Jean M Twenge, PhD (2006) *Generation Me – Why Today's Young Americans Are More Confident, Assertive, Entitled and More Miserable Than Ever Before*, Free Press, New York.
8   In a survey of teens in *USA Today* (2 May, 1999), when asked how much they should be earning at age 30, Gen Y's median answer was US$75,000, when in fact the actual median earnings they could expect on current trends is US$27,000.

3 The expertise trend

It is easy to spot an author in a bookshop. They are the people who, even though they don't look like staff, are busy rearranging the bookshelves. Authors in bookshops are either trying to turn their book sideways (without attracting attention) so the front cover rather than the spine is showing on the shelf, or they are sheepishly moving books from the general shelves to the 'recommended reading' tables at the front of the shop. I know because I too have indulged in this harmless but messy practice (for which I apologize to all Waterstones and Borders London shop staff). The reason we all do it is because we know that despite the hackneyed saying 'you can't judge a book by its cover' there really are only two ways people judge a book – the cover and the title – so we try to maximize a potential reader's exposure to both.

Coming up with a winning cover–title combination can make or break a book. Until now the solution was always to call in the experts. Publishers know what sells and what doesn't. The practice of naming a book and designing its cover follows a tried and tested pattern. First the author suggests a title. Then publishers and their sales people review the suggestion. Does the title feel right for the market? How does it fit with what is currently on the shelves? Having agreed the title, designers get to work on the cover. What look and feel do we need to appeal to the right target audience? Does it work across geographies? Little has changed in the method for some time. Technology has brought in the need to ensure that the title contains key terms that appeal to online searches but that's about as far as things have got. In some cases focus groups and market research have been employed to test out titles and covers but given the margin on books these efforts have been limited.

Stripped of the mystique cherished by expert marketeers the task of naming and covering a book actually includes only three steps – come up with the idea, test it to make sure it works and finally design the cover/typeset the name. In fact, these three steps pretty much describe any business activity – generate an idea, create a product or service and execute your solution. And whilst experts have taken these three steps in much the same way for some time, as much as demographics are wreaking havoc with your experience, technology is wreaking havoc with expertise. To illustrate how profound these changes are, let's take the task of naming and covering a book.

Taking the premise that success in business relies on the ability to harness knowledge in order to optimize transaction costs by leveraging the ambient technology of the time, it is easy to see why we have relied on experts so much. For any business there is always a trade-off between buying expertise from outside or relying on the expertise you have inside your organization. The trade-off is one of managing transaction costs (ie having to manage a vast network of expertise is expensive) versus relying on increased effectiveness (vast markets, despite their high management costs, are always the best way to generate 'perfect' knowledge). But things are changing. Technological advances have ensured that vast markets are now economically viable for even the smallest firm. Technology is now helping us do better and cheaper.

I mentioned that even focus groups are too expensive for the economics of publishing so with this book I tried something different. When I started this project I had three possible titles in mind. Which one would work best? Spurred on by the findings of Ian Ayres in his book *Super Crunchers*,[1] I decided to run three GoogleAds that would come up on the same keyword search. Each ad simply stated one of the proposed titles and the same strap-line was used for all. All other variables being the same, the one that generated the most clicks obviously had the most attractive title.

No longer is it necessary to ask a relatively small (ie affordable) sample of people if they would buy a book. I could actually test with a much larger sample whether people will go to the trouble of purchasing the book. Not only is the sample larger and the activity cheaper but the results are also more powerful. Whilst focus group participants give you an opinion, by clicking on a GoogleAd, my helpers were actually taking an action. They weren't just saying they liked it, they were actually showing me that they liked it enough to interrupt their web surfing. Actions in this case were speaking much louder than words.

Reductions in transaction costs are helping us rethink our business models on a broader scale than ever before, helping us to focus on our core value proposition whilst making everything else cost-efficient. Better than that, by putting prediction markets within the reach of all, technology is helping us redefine expertise.

Prediction markets are predicated on the understanding that the collective judgement of a large group of people can predict the future better than any experts.[2] When Google wants to know how many people will be using Gmail over the next quarter, it adds that to the list of some 275 questions its prediction market has answered since 2005.[3] When Best Buy wants to predict sales it asks its internal market and, some 200 to 400 responses later, non-experts voice their opinion. In these markets people will invest their virtual cash, vote or voice to predict the future. What Best Buy has found, looking back at the markets, is that non-experts tend to be off by only 1 per cent in their predictions, when most experts are off by 7 per cent.

There are also associated benefits in using prediction markets. For example Google found that when the share price is high most of the people in the prediction market tend to be over-optimistic in their forecasts, and with that knowledge Google leaders can make even better predictions. Whenever the answer to a question eludes experts, prediction markets can now be created cheaply and easily. Where will a terrorist strike next? Which of our ongoing projects are most likely to succeed? When will the price of oil change and how high or low will it go? These are all testing questions asked in our testing times that prediction markets have helped to answer. With ever decreasing technology costs, we can now routinely enlist customers (the best experts in the field of their own buying preferences) and others in our creation efforts.

When he published his book *The Art of the Start* in 2004, venture capitalist, original MacIntosh pirate and all round marketing and entrepreneurship guru Guy Kawasaki knew that his book would be judged by its cover, so who better to design it than his potential readership? In partnership with 'istockphoto' (more on them later) he decided to run a competition that generated hundreds of entries. Eventually the cover was settled on by Guy and his team (with 70 other covers displayed on the reverse of the dust jacket of the first edition).

Barry Libert and Jon Spector took what has become known as 'crowdsourcing'[4] a step further when they decided that a book would be even better if written by thousands rather than two experts. Technology helped them connect with a vast community of people who would eventually write a book. *We are Smarter than Me* was published in 2008, counting over a thousand authors, all members of the 'wearesmarterthanme' online community.[5] The task was not only an interesting experiment – it produced one of the most insightful works on mass collaboration and raised some fundamental questions about the nature of leadership and transactions in 'wikinomics'[6] (how do you for example share royalties with authors who might only have contributed a few words versus others who have written an entire chapter?).

Many authors have understood and harnessed the power and wisdom of crowds. When writing his book *Crowdsourcing*,[7] Jeff Howe posted updates on his website and solicited comments. So did Charles Leadbeater when he wrote *We-Think*,[8] exploring the social nature of our new user-generated economy. But let's get back to this book. I mentioned that I decided to test three titles for it. What I didn't mention was that I didn't come up with any of them in the first place. For that, I too relied on a community.

After setting themselves up and securing funding, Kluster's founders realized that the process they used to develop ideas was even more valuable than the ideas for which they had so far got funding. So, without telling anyone (not even their financial backers) they ditched their products and set out to sell their process. Their first foray into becoming a 'user-generated content sourcer and integrator' (my own clumsy way of describing what they do, not theirs) was NameThis. The NameThis proposition is simple.

Anyone can post the description for a new product or service (in my case, a new leadership book). The tribe of volunteers gets to work on naming the new venture. Each tribe member can vote for the names they prefer by allocating them a number of votes (called watts). Watts represent a member's influence as they are earned through participation. After a 48-hour period, Kluster's engine does 'some clever math' (their description, not mine this time) and brings up the three winning entries. In 48 hours I had over 150 names to choose from for this book. Having investigated the services of expert naming firms and looked at the economics of marketing departments whose job it is to fulfil this function in large multinational companies, the US$99 I paid for naming this book redefines what harnessing knowledge to optimize transaction costs means for any business.

What Kluster and other 'social networking technologies' are doing is coordinating a creative activity at costs well below those for the same activity at any time in history. In doing so they are redefining the need for organizations. They are forcing us to question the shape of organizations and, as a result, the relevance of leadership as we know it.

Coordinating activities at the lowest possible cost is the reason organizations exist (hence the name). Bringing all the idea generation, creation and execution activities together under one infrastructure (the organization) reduces the costs associated with coordination. But there are of course costs associated with running an organization.

Take talent costs as an example. You can't recruit all the best people for a task so therefore you need to select the one you think is best at the price you are prepared to pay. You must also consider managerial costs as you need to have someone managing the interactions. On top of that you now have structural costs. You have to create structures that ensure the smooth flow of activities. As long as the total of all these opportunity and hard costs comes to less than you save by having an organization (ie savings on coordination costs), all is well. However, the minute you can deliver more cheaply without incurring these costs, why would anyone in their right mind want to put up with structural, managerial and talent issues?

Let's get back to this book and its cover. What should the cover look like? Let's say I want a picture of a businessman jumping – with sufficient blue sky at the top to position my title.[9] Typing 'businessman' and 'jumping' into the search facility on istockphoto, a website where anyone can post pictures for others to search and purchase, I am now offered 500 pictures of businesspeople in various positions, locations and attires. That so many businesspeople adopt so many different poses in so many different locations is surprising enough, but not as surprising as the search options I can use to narrow my search down. I can now ask for pictures with a portrait or landscape orientation and even search for pictures with a precise area free of any elements within which I will be able to position my text. Doing that leaves me with sixteen choices.[10] I can purchase the picture of my choice for a few dollars depending on its size.

Not only is the price about a tenth of any other stock photo library with a search process that took only a few minutes, but in addition I have access to the photographic skills and imaginative capabilities of an unrestricted number of contributors. No one was shut out of the creation process by a need I had to maintain the price of talent at a minimum by contracting with a restricted number of contributors. Nor did I incur expensive managerial, structural or contractual costs in the process.

If you extrapolate this simple search to business in general you start to realize that the answers to most of your problems might well lie outside your organization in the mind of someone who might be prepared to offer them to you at a tenth of the cost that would be incurred by your own experts. You can pretty much solve all your problems instantly, irrespective of whether you have in-house capability and capacity or had ever thought about needing an answer in the future. In addition this ubiquitous technology removes the need for planning, making your creation process more agile (ie able to adapt and change nimbly).

My guess is that we have all experienced what Harvard Law School Professor Yochai Benkler describes when he talks about the mobile phone having abolished the need to plan. As soon as you got your first mobile phone you started to say things like 'I tell you what, how about I call you when I'm done here and then we can see what we'll do'. Prior to mobile communication you would have had to make a plan and aim to stick to it. 'I tell you what, I will meet you tonight at the station by the newspaper stand at half past six when I come out of the office' would have been the exchange you had in the morning prior to setting off for work. If a deadline had emerged, the plan would have evaporated and with it the goodwill of the person you were supposed to meet and had not been able to contact. This kind of flexibility in business is priceless. This lack of 'need to plan' also means that you need less managerial time to coordinate. The requirements for a leader to complete the coordination task start to look a bit shaky. The talent, managerial and structure costs suddenly disappear almost as fast as the opportunities appear.

Today's technology is putting the world of co-creation on steroids. What has become known as 'distributed co-creation' – the bringing together of talent from numerous sources outside the organizational boundaries – is only in its infancy but growing at an exponential rate. The T-shirt quote that began Chapter 1 is only one example of it.

Threadless, the company behind the T-shirt, relies on its users' community to generate designs that other members vote on and eventually purchase. Open source software was perhaps the best-known precursor to the developing movement. As more companies reconfigure their supply chain to rely on expertise beyond their organizational walls they will increasingly come to rely on a happy band of amateur experts (many call them 'prosumers', for professional consumers). Already, whilst traditional websites are growing by about 20 per cent a year, user-generated media sites are growing at about 100 per cent a year.[11] The drive for co-creation illustrated by user-generated content is relentless. The often quoted example of Wikipedia, which in fewer than seven years has grown to be the world's biggest encyclopaedia with more than six million articles in over 250 languages, is but the tip of the iceberg. The very act of creating a product or service is no longer the preserve of a closed organizational system of experts. As the world reconfigures the make-up of expertise, that of individual leaders could become irrelevant. To make matters worse our next trend puts a multiplier effect on the expertise trend. Get ready for the attention trend.

The 30 second recap

Organizations exist to overcome the contractual costs of managing multiple relationships. Their very existence however also means that some people who may be able to add value are also excluded from them (ie you just can't recruit everyone). As technology develops, it is now possible for networks to create value in a much more inclusive, and therefore powerful, way than organizations can.

As a result, the expertise that drives organizational value now resides in a network of relationships outside the managerial reach of the organization itself. This raises questions about the very value of organizations and, by association, their leaders.

Notes

1   I Ayres (2007) *Super Crunchers: How anything can be predicted*, John Murray.
2   James Surowiecki (2004) *The Wisdom of Crowds*, Little, Brown.
3   *The McKinsey Quarterly* (2008) Number 2.
4   Jeff Howe (2008) *Crowdsourcing: Why the Power of the Crowd Is Driving the Future of Business*, Crown Business.

5   Barry Libert and Jon Spector (2007) *We Are Smarter Than Me: How to Unleash the Power of Crowds in Your Business*, Wharton School Publishing.

6   Wikinomics is the term coined by Don Tapscott and Anthony Williams to describe the economy of online collaboration in their book *Wikinomics* (published by Portfolio in 2006).

7   Jeff Howe (2008) *Crowdsourcing: Why the Power of the Crowd Is Driving the Future of Business*, Crown Business.

8   Charles Leadbeater (2008) *We-think: The Power of Mass Creativity*, Profile Books.

9   At the time of writing this line the cover for the book has not been decided upon and I do hope no one at the design agency will be sad enough to ever suggest having a businessman jumping as the right image for the cover. But stick with me here, I am trying to make a point.

10   If you're interested my choice would have been a picture by Viorika exclusive to istockphoto with the file number 6507087.

11   Jacques Bughin, Michael Chui and Brad Johnson (2008) The next step in open innovation, *The McKinsey Quarterly*, online edition number 2.

4 The attention trend

On the morning of 1 August 2005, former US Vice President, Nobel Prize winner and, for some, 2000 President Elect Al Gore was about to start a revolution. It had nothing to do with climate change.

At midnight on the morning of 1 August 2005, the cable television network founded by Al Gore and businessman Joel Hyatt went on air. This was not just any new channel. Marrying so-called old and new media, it was the first full 24-hour user-generated network. The short three- to seven-minute programmes it features (called pods) are all created by users (called VC2 Producers). Anyone can submit a pod, on any subject matter, to the Current website where registered users vote to decide which they would like to see broadcast. The Current programming department makes a final decision based on these votes. In addition to VC2-submitted content, Current also features 'Current:News', which follows stories submitted and voted on by the online community.

This 'democratizer' (Al Gore's description) of content was to pick up an Emmy award in September 2007. Along with the United States, the channel is also available in the United Kingdom and Italy. Its appeal to viewers aged 16 to 34 (darlings of advertisers) as well as the distributed co-creation of content makes Current the standard-bearer of the demographic and expertise trends. But more than that, Current is also a destination where people go to invest their discretionary effort (ie the effort they have left after they have spent their energy on essential tasks). And this is what makes Current a key player in our third trend, the attention trend.

The average e-mail user will receive 65,000 messages this year alone.[1] More than 300,000 books are published every year.[2] The average weekday edition of *The New York Times* contains more information than someone would have come across in his or her lifetime in 17th-century England.[3] Forty exabytes (4×10^{19}) of unique information is produced in a year – more than was produced in the previous 5,000 years. A typical supermarket stocks around 40,000 items.[4] Pieces of direct mail to hit letterboxes in the United States every year number 87.2 billion.[5] You can access more than 2 billion web pages. Internet traffic doubles every hundred days.[6] It is estimated that the internet is 500 times larger[7] than the 91 million daily Google searches[8] can ever show. So where do you focus? Where do you go for answers? Or is the only answer to just switch off?

The answer to that last question is probably the most worrying for leaders. With 48 million avatars (online representations of individuals) currently roaming the web,[9] 10 per cent of whom do so for more than 10 hours a day, MMORPGs (massively multiplayer online role-playing games) and associated virtual worlds might well be in the process of designing a new reality. OK so that's a pretty bold claim – which you may now be looking to reject on analytical grounds alone. So let's just think about it for a second. Let's get back to Current.

The interesting thing here is not that a new generation is co-creating content, but rather why it is doing it, when so much content is already available. It all comes down to effort – the effort people decide to spend on things and the effort you spend on attracting them to spend effort on these things. These are the two important variables in this new trend.

In these days of 'attention warfare' (ie being constantly under attack by messages) people whose attention is limited learn to focus on the things they decide are important to them. That is to say that they only allocate the limited effort they have to specific things they deem are worth their while and switch off their attention from other things.

The other important point is that some people are better at creating things that attract people than others. The key reason why so many social networking and virtual technologies have become so appealing is that they mimic our normal everyday social lives much better than any of the organizations we have created.

The attention trend reminds me of a scene in the blockbuster movie *The March of the Penguins*, charting the breeding seasons of a penguin colony, when the mothers return from their hunting trip and call out for their offspring. In the most amazing display of nature's wonder, amidst a scene of chaos, where thousands of penguins, adults and their young, shout at the tops of their voices, mothers and children are always, without fail, reunited. Amongst the thousands of voices both recognize the voice of their tribe. In 'penguin world', having a recognizable voice is a clear way to cut through the noise and attract those who belong to a group.

The same is true of our world. We recognize the call of the tribe to which we want to belong. For people this means restricting listening to the voices we trust and can easily recognize. For organizations, being better at creating things that attract people's attention is not a function of cleverness, but rather a function of focus. In a world that is already crowded, if you try to be all things to all people your message becomes so diluted that it loses the capability to stand out above the noise. If you have a specific way of saying or doing things you suddenly stand for something loud enough to attract the people who matter. It may well mean that you attract fewer people, but these people will be devoted people. Just as the baby penguin on the frozen ice cap hears its parents' voices amidst the cacophony of thousands of other penguins' cries, your potential audience (attuned to a specific tone) will hear your voice and find you. Incidentally, what is true of real penguins is also true of virtual ones – my children will always recognize the call of Club Penguin!

The trouble is that the cries of organizations are becoming less and less audible as they become less and less distinguishable. People are growing deaf to your efforts to be heard. Indications that this trend has already started are demonstrated by Current. People no longer rely on traditional sources (in the case of news, that would be journalists) to make sense of their world. They are prepared to belong to and further the cause of communities that bring coherence to their world. In so doing they construct a digital identity that they can control and through which they can apply filters. Traditional organizations no longer fit that model.

Already online communities and social networks are growing beyond the size we ever thought possible. MySpace's membership has gone from 20 million people in 2005 to 225 million in 2008.[10] That's an average annual growth rate of 513 per cent. Facebook, the second most-trafficked social media site with more than 150 million active users[11] grew at 550 per cent during the same period. LinkedIn's networking platform grows annually at a rate of 82 per cent. You may still see this as a side issue but it means that, were they countries, MySpace would be the fifth biggest country in the world after China, India, the United States and Indonesia whilst its neighbouring country Facebook would be the eighth biggest, making it the biggest in the European Union.[12] Membership in MMORPG grew from nothing in 1997 to about 16 million by 2008; at the current growth rate there will be over 30 million players by 2013.[13] In country terms that means that the 39th biggest country by 2013 will be a virtual gaming world inhabited by avatars. Revenues of MMORPG hit US$662 million in China alone in 2007 – an increase of about 70 per cent over 2005.[14] Second Life (the virtual world) has over 14 million residents who spend an average of 30 hours a month online. This means that the 65th biggest country of a list of 221[15] is a land that only exists on the servers of Linden Lab (the company behind Second Life).

So yes, people may be turning up for work but they are no longer investing all their efforts in your cause. Your efforts at attracting them using the tools and levers you have always used (eg reward, recognition, threats and rules) will no longer engage them to the extent that they recognize you as an integral part of their world. In these circumstances how do you leverage talent when no one hears your cries for help?

As leaders our role is not only to get people to do something, it is to get them to do more than they thought possible. We want them to allocate their discretionary effort to our cause. Our reliance on roles and rules and economic incentives to achieve these ends has been to the detriment of the moral and social obligations that make us release that discretionary effort. That in itself would not be a problem if we had nowhere else to turn. But, as technology enables the creation of much more targeted communal experience in a way organizations could never replicate, the efforts put in by leaders to win the fight for attention will be largely wasted.

Faced with this trend some organizations are multiplying their communication efforts. They try (sometimes successfully) to use new channels to reach us. But what the attention trend demonstrates is not so much that we need to be more intelligent and credible about where we find people but much more importantly, it will shape what we say to them once we have found a place where they might listen.

After three trends you might safely reason that things are not as bad as they seem. After all, your leadership position still means that you are in charge. Your desire to create value along with your power to do so should see you win the day. This is where our fourth and final shift comes in. When everything that has made you successful is crumbling, there will be little hope in clinging to your leadership power to see you through as the democratic shift is about to make that irrelevant too. In many ways this is probably the easiest of the challenges to explain, yet it is the one with the most profound consequences at it severs the final cord that made the leader's role relevant.

The 30 second recap

As human beings we are bombarded by messages and information. Unable to make sense of them all, we look to communities to help us focus. We rely on a few brands. We read only a couple of newspapers. We follow the same blogs. This selectiveness is our way of cutting through the information clutter and the demands on our attention.

Whilst organizations used to form part of that network of attention, a collection of social and informational networks is coming to replace them as a source of coherence and cohesion for people. The reason is simple; they replicate more closely the way we seek engagement than organizations have been able to achieve through their narrow focus on roles, rules and economic incentives, rather than on individuals and their sense of moral and social obligations.

Notes

1   R S Wurman (2001) *Information Anxiety 2*, Que.
2   Thomas H Davenport (2002) *The Attention Economy*, Harvard Business School Publishing.
3   R S Wurman (2001) *Information Anxiety 2*, Que.
4   Thomas H Davenport (2002) *The Attention Economy*, Harvard Business School Publishing.
5   Thomas H Davenport (2002) *The Attention Economy*, Harvard Business School Publishing.
6   Thomas H Davenport (2002) *The Attention Economy*, Harvard Business School Publishing.
7   M Liedtke (2000) *Study: Internet Bigger Than We Think*, Associated Press.
8   Data obtained on 18 July 2008 from searchenginewatch.com.
9   Data courtesy of Phil White of mmogdata.voig.com. Please note that the data change all the time as, much like our own, the online universe has been known to expand and contract but even with these changes the vastness of space remains.
10   K Kelleher (2008) 'MySpace and Friends Need to Make Money. And Fast', *Wired magazine*, March.
11   http://stanford.facebook.com/press/info.php?statistics (January 2009).
12   http://en.wikipedia.org/wiki/List_of_countries_by_population.
13   Bruce Sterling Woodcock, *An Analysis of MMOG Subscription Growth* [Online] MMOGCHART.COM.

14 Michael R Polin (2007) *China Online Gaming; MMORPG/Casual Revenues and Business Models* [Online] InvestorIdeas.com.

15 www.secondlife.com's own data (July 2008).

5 The democratic trend

Given that 1 in 10 Europeans has been conceived on an Ikea mattress and that Ikea's products are ubiquitous in every country they enter, probability would suggest that wherever you live on the globe you have come across and visited the blue and yellow temple for the home. Whether shopping at the new store in Novosibirsk, Siberia, where Ikea is at the forefront of the development of shopping malls or at the Brooklyn store in New York, which Ikea managed to open after numerous concessions to the neighbourhood, the experience will be the same.

You first need to fight the traffic to get there, only to begin the somewhat schizophrenic experience of Ikea shopping; schizophrenic because Ikea requires you to adopt as many different roles as there are stages in the experience. You are the interior designer arranging products together. You are the consumer savouring your meatballs. You become the storeroom picker carrying your goods, prior to acting as the transport manager loading stuff into the car. Ultimately, as Ikea outsourced their factory to your living room floor, you will then become either a master builder or product designer depending on your patience and skills (let's face it, who hasn't managed in their time to transform a 'billy' bookcase into something that better resembles a bed?). You will then face the judgement of the quality control department (roles played with relish by your family members or friends).

We are facing the 'Ikeazation' of our world. Our economies are starting to look like giant Ikea stores where people go from one role to another depending on their skills, passions – and ultimately demand. In these schizophrenic times, the idea that there are such things as employees or customers no longer satisfactorily represents the complexity of the economic activity. As organizations change shape, positional power (ie the power leaders hold due to their positions) is being eroded to the point of irrelevance. The democratic trend is the logical conclusion of the other three. A new generation eager to serve with the tools of co-creation at its disposal and the will to create communities of interest was always likely to demand the right to participate.

That this trend has already started is beyond debate. The US department of labour estimates that today's students will have had 10 to 14 jobs by the age of 38. Already today, one in four US employees is working for an organization they have been at for less than a year. Half of all employees in the United States have worked for their company for less than five years.[1] The transient nature of employment is making it a lot harder for leaders to have an enforceable psychological contract with their employees. With these conditions we can't blame anyone for wanting to look after number one. But the democratic trend goes much further. The 'Ikeazation' of work is not just about the fast change in the number of jobs people have over a period of time, but also about the organization for which they work.

Anyone who has ever worked in a so-called matrix organization will be familiar with the difficulty one experiences when faced with conflicting priorities dictated by differing leaders. The main functions fulfilled by lines on an organizational chart have always been to direct focus and attention. That had a clear advantage, but also an inbuilt disadvantage. The advantage is that clarity can easily be delivered. The disadvantage is that its narrow focus does not sit well with the demands of a dynamic environment. The matrix, with its multiple lines, was supposed to increase the number of areas one would care about. Uncomfortable with the lack of control engendered by lack of singular focus, leaders struggle to make things work. Now imagine a world where the lines are not only blurred, but they have disappeared.

Already you might have experienced this world when dealing with the growing world of what I call 'peripheral' staff (ie people not in full-time employment contracts inside your organization – part-time employees, temporary staff, contractors or consultants). With the changing shape of the mature economies away from manufacturing and into service, that world has grown. Between 1982 and 1992 the number of temporary employees in the United States tripled.[2] Since 1995 temporary employment has grown three times faster than traditional employment in the United States.[3]

In that world contracts might buy you some effort but contracts alone cannot give you the discretionary effort of people on whose attention multiple demands are placed. You have had to rely on something other than your position or contractual obligations if you wanted to see them investing themselves in your task. Of course most leaders would recognize that this is the case with any employee, but most would also admit that the situation is somewhat easier with full-time staff. As distributed co-creation grows, the need to rely on something other than contracts and social power to fully engage others becomes paramount. The logical conclusion of the 'Ikeazation' of the job market is the birth of a powerful force in the economy – the free agents.

You would have thought that given the importance placed on it by economists, policy makers and business in general, data on employment trends would be easy to come by and analyse. You would probably be wrong on both counts. There is a lot of data out there but analysing it is somewhat difficult when you are looking at free agency.[4] What makes such analyses difficult is that it is in fact very hard to classify occupation in any meaningful way when it comes to free agency. For example actors who are currently filming are employed but become unemployed between films. Consultants who are working on projects are employed but unemployed when in between projects.

Indeed, I am employed all year round by my own company (there is something ironic about using the word company when you work alone). This makes me employed for statistical purposes, but self-employed for all other intents and purposes. In fact, as a self-employed person, can I be considered to be working when writing in the same way as I work when I consult on a client's project? When you consider that the US department of labour still sees the world of employment as being divided between agricultural and non-agricultural employment you understand that there is some way to go before we can make sense of all statistics.

Using realistic and conservative estimates, counting only people who clearly are free agents, we can estimate that currently one in four US citizens is a free agent. This means that one in four US citizens have no boss to answer to on an organizational chart.[5] Add to that number the peripheral staff I mentioned earlier and you see how the use of positional power is no longer helping anyone. Now, project that into the future and the estimates are that up to half the US working population will be free agents of one kind or another within the next four years. On current outsourcing and contracting trends alone we can safely estimate that by that time, well over half the population will no longer work in a traditional employment relationship. That's a lot of people who couldn't care less about leaders' positional power, especially when you consider that the ones left will probably have so many dotted lines by then that you will have had to come up with differentiated engagement strategies.

If you still doubt that this trend exists just consider that, in the cradle of most of today's advances that is California, two out of three workers currently hold non-traditional positions, hidden by employment statistics.[6] Is this a global trend? That's harder to say as figures are more difficult to come by and to compare globally, but the trend is present to a lesser or larger extent in most developed economies.

The 'Ikeazation' of work is placing a democratic demand on the organization. Yes you can lead us, but only if we vote you capable of doing so. Let's not confuse a world of free agency with a world of abundance. Some may think the trend will slow in a downturn when people want to keep hold of their jobs. The truth is that, even without accounting for the people who are forced into free agency through being laid off, the trend is unlikely to slow down. This is not just about people opting out or becoming entrepreneurs, the democratic trend is about people no longer being in your direct span of control. Organizations today are starting to resemble webs of relationships with multiple organizational hubs. Even if you still have a direct team reporting to you and they don't have a choice about this, you still have to get the best out of consultants, customers, partners and other agencies upon which your success depends.

Devoid of positional power, in the words of Professors Rob Goffee and Gareth Jones of the London Business School, 'why should anyone be led by you?'

Taken together, these four trends form a coherent whole. They foretell a world where relationships between followers and leaders will need to be different from what they are today if they are to be productive. Yet, for every worrying facet of change there are opportunities. Whilst this work is making the way we lead today irrelevant, it is also a world crying out for leadership.

Just as subjects living under the rules of monarchies proclaim 'long live the new monarch' when one passes away, we need to understand that the time for a new type of leadership is upon us. The demographic, expertise, attention and democratic trends herald a day of reckoning for a dying form of leadership, but they do not altogether make the practice of leadership redundant. Our challenge is to understand the communities that will form the new business landscape and the way they are best engaged for the delivery of an economic objective. There is little need to continue to get better at what we do when what we do is no longer what is needed.

So, given these four trends, let's try to understand what lies at the root of engagement in the new landscape. Once we understand this, we can turn to our role in making it happen. Penguins started us off on our journey and it is a terrorist duck we need to turn to for the answers that will enable us to progress along our path.

The 30 second recap

We are all becoming familiar with the so-called dotted lines of matrix organizations. We also all know how difficult it is to work within them. Now imagine living in a world of dotted lines. That world is the one the democratic trend is preparing for us. Numerous forms of free agency are appearing. An organization is now a complex system of relationships most of which sit outside a leader's span of control.

In the democratic world, leaders are no longer an accident of birth. We can choose whom to follow. We even get to vote whenever we want. In this world, the leader never gets to call the election.

Devoid of positional power, leaders need to find a new way of engaging people. When the social, intellectual and informational capital of an organization no longer sits inside a leader's span of control, democracy takes over.

Taken together our four trends (demographic, expertise, attention and democratic) spell the death of leadership as we know it (check out the initials – D.E.A.D)!

Notes

1 Employment data obtained from www.bls.gov releases.
2 Lonnie Golden (1996) The expansion of temporary help employment in the US, 1982–1992: A test of alternative economic explanation, *Applied Economics*, **28**, pp 1127–91.
3 James Aley (1995) Where the Jobs Are, *Fortune*, 18 September.
4 Daniel H Pink (2001) *Free Agent Nation*, Warner Business Books, Chapter 1.
5 Michelle Coulin (2000) And Now the Just-in-time Employee, *Business Week*, 28 August.
6 Kenneth Howe (1999) Workforce Revolution in California; Only One in Three Holds Traditional Job, Study Finds, *San Francisco Chronicle*, 6 September.

6 Pay or play?

In December 2005, proudly sporting a red Santa hat and blue shirt, Philip Linden stood amongst his people. The crowd, gathered for an early winter holiday party, was looking forward to a joyful celebration of their ever growing community. Seeing Philip dance around the roaring bonfire, they couldn't have anticipated what he was about to say. 'This seems about as good a time as any to tell you that I am turning over names to the FBI'[1] was not the festive message anyone had expected. Philip Linden is the name of Philip Rosedale's avatar (CEO of Linden Lab, the company behind Second Life). His words were surprising but greeted with virtual cheers by virtual residents toasting virtual marshmallows around the virtual fire. They were also the logical conclusion to a series of unwelcome events. Second Life (SL) was under attack and one view united the community – it was all the Duck's fault.

To be fair to the Duck no one knows for sure what his involvement was and he denies any wrongdoing. To the community though, his name had become shorthand for all that it hates. To SL residents, the name Plastic Duck (or Gene Replacement, his other in-world name) resonates in the same way as the names Al Capone or Lee Harvey

Oswald do in the real world. They are somehow ghastly but immensely fascinating.

Plastic Duck began his online road to fame as a member of the W-Hat, a group of SL residents intent on creating havoc in the peaceful world. In Second Life people who cause trouble are known as 'griefers' and whilst, admittedly, the W-Hat leadership describe their group as a 'non-griefing' group intent on satire, the line between humour and offence is pretty blurred. And when you know that its members have been linked to the recreation of a virtual flaming World Trade Center (complete with smashed planes, smoke and falling bodies), then, suddenly, our story's funny overtones start to turn sinister. Yet, following the enforced closure by Linden Lab in 2006 of 60 accounts linked to a W-Hat splinter group called 'Voted 5', things have calmed down. Even though members still drive around in a van proclaiming 'W-Hat Cyber Terrorists Since 2004', they have certainly changed their act. Their activities now appear limited to following people around mocking them with puppets. Still, it's hard for the community to be objective or forgiving when it comes to Plastic Duck and in 2005 it was impossible. He had been accused of such deeds as denigrating the furry community (a group of residents who like to appear as animals), spamming penis images across the world, sexually harassing female residents, hiring residents to post negative feedback on others and stealing scripts of other people's creations to post on the web. As a rap sheet it makes for pretty tasteless reading, but what does it tell us about the DEAD trends?

Plastic Duck's creator is 21-year-old Patrick Sapinski, a student from Ajaz, Ontario. In 2005, aged 17, Patrick, confined to his bed by what was later diagnosed as Crohn's disease, discovered Second Life. Second Life was a way for him to socialize, to make friends, to play pranks. It was a way for a bedridden student to do, from his bedroom, the things healthy students plan from their college dorms. Quickly, Patrick was attracted to the shenanigans of the W-Hat.

Like most teenagers, Patrick wanted to test the limits of his community. Whilst anything is possible in the virtual world of SL (where you can fly and walk under water), the world itself is amazingly similar to the real world. Far from being some strange planet, the majority of people display very real-world-like behaviours. It is telling that in a world that never gets cold and where it never rains, most people's first activity is to build themselves a house. Patrick's mission was to disrupt the status quo – to make what he saw as a boring place more fun. What led him to trouble (fast amassing a double-digit rap sheet from Linden Lab) was when he was accused of going beyond disrupting the minds of inhabitants to disrupting the world itself.

In SL, inhabitants can build any object they want by just writing some computer code. Plastic Duck is accused of scripting objects responsible for crashing the world itself. These objects self-replicated at such a rate that Linden Lab's servers could not cope with the exponential multiplication. Eventually, the grid (the platform on which the world is built) crashed. That's when Philip Linden decided that virtual world terrorism was a real world crime. SL argued that crashing the grid was like any denial-of-service attack on an internet web page and therefore a real world crime. That moment was the first sign of our trends crossing over to the real world. And this is why the Duck matters to our story.

Human beings need three basic food groups to survive – protein, fats and carbohydrates. Eat more or less of any one group than you should and your health suffers. Organizations are no different. They too rely on three basic food groups – control, structure and resources. In this context, the Duck is death by chocolate. He is what happens when organizations become indisposed. He is the bad bacteria that spoils your organizational gut. He is the gastroenteritis of leadership. He is the inevitable outcome of the DEAD trends. Let's work on that one.

To be effective, organizations rely on control. They need to be able to control input, throughput and output to fulfil the organizational mission. They need not only to be able to control resources but to control events, for anything unplanned is likely to be undesirable. Without control organizations deviate from their paths. Control is primarily achieved through a hierarchy of roles. Roles give clarity. They legitimize control by laying down an operational structure. Control and structure enable the effective deployment of resources.

Without resources (human and financial) organizations do not exist. A healthy organization is one where the three elements are balanced. The way the DEAD trends threaten the effectiveness and legitimacy of leaders is by destabilizing that balance.

The demographic trend coupled with the attention shift are a direct threat to control. You cannot control either what you do not understand or what doesn't want to be controlled. The combination of the expertise trend and the democratic trend means that the legitimacy of structures (which relies on either knowledge or willing adoption of roles, and preferably both) is no longer present. The rejection of current organizational forms forced by the demographic and attention trends mixed with the loss of leaders' positional power as a result of the democratic and expertise trends threatens the order necessary for success.

The Duck and his kind became an integral part of the organizational narrative, intent on destroying it. On 1 April 2008 (a date, I am convinced, chosen at random and without a hint of irony), when EdMarkey Alter, better known in the real world as Congressman Ed Markey (D-MA) chaired the first ever congressional hearing simultaneously held in the US Congress and SL,[2] Philip Rosendale confirmed that he had indeed asked the FBI to investigate denial of service attacks. Yet he also stated that he was confident that the community could police itself. But how? This is important not just to the future of Second Life and its inhabitants but to the future of leadership. If the trends are breaking down control, how can order, necessary for success, emerge from the chaos created by lost teenagers in need of kicks? When control, hierarchies and resources disintegrate, how can we consistently deliver the organization's mission? How can we create self-discipline within the organization? How can we achieve coordination and control without structural hierarchies?

What we need to understand is the nature of relationships between people involved in mass collaboration processes once the structural layers of a hierarchy are removed. To further our understanding, however, I can't just rely on a duck; I also need you to know something about pigs and chickens.

A pig and a chicken are walking down a road. The chicken looks at the pig and says, 'Hey, why don't we open a restaurant?' The pig looks back at the chicken: 'Good idea, what should we call it?' The chicken thinks about it for a minute and suggests, 'How about "Ham and Eggs"?' 'I don't think so,' says the pig, 'because that would mean that I am committed but you'd only be involved.' This joke may not be the funniest you ever heard but it tells us something about the nature of roles in organizations and why the DEAD trends demand a new perspective on the execution process.

In 1986, Hirotaka Takeuchi, now dean of the Graduate School of International Corporate Strategy at Hitotsubashi University in Tokyo, developed a new model for agile software development with Ikujiro Nonaka, based on their work on tacit knowledge accumulation. The process recognized that traditional sequential approaches required each function involved in the process to work on one project at a time, passing the baton over (like in a relay race) to others as the project progressed. This not only slowed down projects but ensured limited access to knowledge at any one time. They decided that a process more attuned to a game of rugby where the team 'tries to go the distance as a unit, passing the ball back and forth' would be more appropriate to the development and sharing of knowledge critical to software development.

What Takeuchi and Nonaka were defining as the limitations of classic software development projects are also the limitations of any organizational efforts relying on hierarchically-dictated resource allocation (in fact their pioneering work in the field of knowledge management further reinforces this). As the trends attack our organizational models, the insights Takeuchi and Nonaka had offer us the beginning of a solution to our coordination issue. In 1990, Peter DeGrace and Leslie Hulet Stahl, in their book *Wicked Problems, Righteous Solutions*, using the rugby term mentioned in the original article by Takeuchi and Nonaka,[3] referred to the approach as 'scrum'. That's where the chicken and pig come in. In line with the story, the scrum approach identifies two types of roles in any process – pigs and chickens.

The pigs are committed to the project. They have 'their bacon on the line' so to speak. The chickens, on the other hand, are involved because they are interested in its benefits. Both are important but already we can see how their contributions, and therefore their desires and accountabilities, might differ. The pigs are running the scrum. They are the builders and doers. The chickens provide impetus through their desires and needs but it is not in their interest to get in the way of the process. The system self-regulates through the reciprocity it offers. There are some interesting parallels to explore between scrum roles and non-hierarchical communal roles.

There are three pig roles identified by Takeuchi and Nonaka. Product owners are the ones who shape the product on the basis of what the customer wants. Facilitators are the ones whose job it is to remove anything that might stand in the way of the team fulfilling its objectives. And finally there is the team itself. Team members are the people who will complete the necessary tasks to bring the project to completion.

When we look at mass collaboration communities, and social networks that underpin organizations, we can identify similar roles.

The product owner is the one I call master. **Masters** are the voice of the community. They are dignitaries who define the direction. They are the judges and often jury of communal behaviour. They are critical to the organizational experience as they are custodians of its future. They are the ones who, through first mover advantage, reputation or sheer determination of contribution, have seen themselves elevated to this position by the community.

The role of facilitator is fulfilled by the people I call shapers. **Shapers** are the community's committee members. They are engaged and active. Their existence is defined by both what the community stands for and the needs of our next role – the participants.

Participants are the team of the community. They are the bees in the communal hive fulfilling the maintenance tasks. They are the people for whom the community is shaped and in turn they provide meaning and *raison d'être* to the community through their actions.

Now if these are the pigs then who are the chickens? Who are the ones who are involved but not committed? Here again, Takeuchi and Nonaka identify three roles. **Users** are the ones the project exists to serve. They will ultimately use the software being built. The second role is the one of stakeholder. **Stakeholders** are not necessarily the same as users. They may be the customer buying the product for example. Finally come the **managers** who, unlike facilitators, do not get involved in managing the project, but rather set up the environment within which the project can take place.

If we look at organizations with social rather than organizational structures and devolved control (the SL of this world for example), we again find some parallels.

In this case the group of users are best termed as dependents. **Dependents** identify themselves as members of the community but only in so far as the community's existence provides an emotional attraction for them. They do not actively contribute to the community, but it provides sufficient meaning for them to transact with it. So, in the case of Second Life, they would be the casual visitors who build their own territory but do not shape the community beyond the boundaries of their homes.

The role of manager is taken on by the overall **platform creator**. For example, by providing the grid on which Second Life sits, Linden Lab constructs the environment for communal expression.

Of course, in every community, there will be rebels. **Rebels** are interesting because they oscillate between the chicken and pig roles. Their mindset is that of the chicken, whilst their motivation is that of the pig. The Duck is a good example of a rebel who defines himself through his dislike of the community (I know this whole thing is starting to sound like a menagerie)! His efforts at sabotage to destabilize the community make him paradoxically highly dependent on its existence. His very presence unites dependents whilst energizing masters.

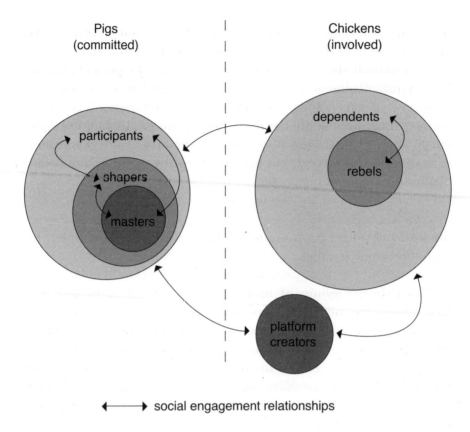

Figure 6.1   Social engagement architecture in mass collaboration

There are three insights the chicken and the pig nomenclature can offer us, see Figure 6.1 above.

The first is that, when it comes to a creation effort, the organization as we know it is, in fact, more akin to a dependent (a chicken role) than a master (a pig role). It is involved rather than committed to the creation task. In the case of Second Life for example, Linden Lab is in fact a chicken to the pigs that are building the community. Remember George and Club Penguin. This explains the source of his discomfort. If he is the pig building the community it is hard to be told by the chicken what you should do. That's the point of the scrum. Chickens clearly matter but they must be excluded from the pigs' work. Of course this doesn't mean to say that the organization is not important, since without the organization (the chicken) there are no reasons for the project to exist. But what we must emphasize at this stage is that the organization (the platform owner), per se, is not *more* important than the other roles.

The second insight is that roles do not relate to each other in a functional, linear way (as in 'passing the baton'). The relationship between roles in a creation effort is not linear. Linear functional relationships are not a true representation of how work takes place and in fact slow down any creative endeavour.

The final insight is one of numbers. Whilst pigs are critical, they are less numerous than chickens. So who is most important? Who should we pay attention to as we progress towards the new world of business? Surely we should follow the money. Go for the ones who have the most value. Allow me to poke you on to this next stage. Nothing like a good poke to help us understand how value flows through mass collaboration processes and what that means for organizations.

When many of us were small we were told that poking people was not a good thing to do. The practice of prodding, even a friend, with your finger to cause nuisance was generally frowned upon as being rude. That all changed the day Facebook was launched. For those of you still to discover the at once mesmerizing and infuriating community that is Facebook, it is an online social network where you invite your friends to connect with you and share pictures, news and the like.

What makes Facebook fascinating is the vast collection of widgets available. Widgets are small programs that can be plugged into your profile on the page. These can do anything from providing a graphical representation of your network to displaying the top friends you communicate with most and offering you a daily, targeted horoscope. One of the most popular (by way of number of downloads) widgets on Facebook is SuperPoke.

In Facebook when you want to tell someone you have identified them as a potential friend you can click a button to poke them. Poking them means that they receive a note of your existence and can decide if they want to poke back, become your friend or alternatively spend the rest of their day wondering who the stalking freak is who poked them. SuperPoke goes one step further by offering any number of actions you can perform on your friends beyond the mere poke. With SuperPoke you can 'blow a kiss', 'cuddle', 'rock the grannie panties' or even 'go Chuck Norris on' your friends.

The practice may be puerile but it becomes a whole lot more serious when you realize that giant investment firms, Fidelity and T Rowe Price, paid US$50 million for a 9.1 per cent stake in Slide, the San Francisco-based company responsible for the SuperPoke widget.[4] That, in one fell swoop, valued the company at more than half a billion dollars (enough to rock anyone's panties in my book). There are two reasons why Slide is of interest here.

The first reason has to do with our attention trend. The growth of social networks is such that online activity is an exponentially growing potential source of revenue. Online search, the activity currently accounting for a large share of online advertising revenue, only accounts for about 6 per cent of online activities. So why such an extraordinary valuation for Slide? After all, surely the actual social network (ie Facebook) is the one on which the value rests? The answer lies in the demographic trend. MySpace is replacing my place as the meeting place for advertisers' key demographics. And guess what, Slide's widgets are present on MySpace or any other open social networking sites, enabling you to poke to your heart's content. Viewed in this context, Slide becomes a critical tool to connect to key demographics across numerous platforms. But there is an even more important reason why Slide is valued so highly and that reason gives us a clue about how roles will interact in a post-DEAD trend world.

Slide's CEO, Max Levchin of PayPal fame, which he co-founded and sold to eBay in 2002 for US$1.5 billion, explains the success of his widget factory (now the largest in the world with over 50 million users) like this: 'The metrics for success,' says Levchin, 'are going to trend away from who can provide the most reach toward who is paid the most attention.'[5]

In Levchin's mind, if users of the internet are involved primarily in social activities on the web, page view (the normal metric for success) is no longer viable. The new metric of choice according to Levchin is engagement. Engagement is expressed as a much broader measure than click through or page view. Engagement is about what makes people tick and how they interact with the rest of the world. And that is what Levchin can measure. Behavioural data are much more important than activity. Whilst he may have a tough time persuading an entire industry that has relied on activity as its main measure of effectiveness, there are signs that the industry is catching on. Google introducing a cost-per-action rather than per click option for advertisers and the mighty global information and media company Nielsen looking at 'engagement mapping' are but two examples of the trend. On the basis that our concern here is how to get people involved and engaged when they no longer have to be, engagement seems to be the measure we too should be concerned about. At this stage let me introduce the 1 per cent rule.

In their book *Citizen Marketers*,[6] Uber Marketers Ben McConnell and Jackie Huba (the people who coined the term 'customer evangelist'), introduce us to the piece of analysis they call the 1 per cent rule. Discovered after lengthy data analysis, the 1 per cent rule states that in every online community (eg Wikipedia, Facebook, YouTube…) the number of people who actively create or contribute content (ie the pigs) is roughly 1 per cent of the number of visitors (ie 99 per cent are chickens). It seems that the Pareto principle loved by business people (ie 20 per cent of our customers contribute 80 per cent of our profit) gets diluted online.

The current rules of engagement are segmentation driven. Segmentation is data driven. We look at consumption data for customers and performance data for employees. As any financial adviser will tell you that past performance is no guarantee of future return, we then try to assess potential (using more and more intricate psychosocial and demographic tools, both incidentally still wholly based on historical data). The analysis invariably reveals that around 20 per cent of customers and employees are worth caring about. So we devise an engagement strategy to nurture, cajole and coerce their discretionary spend or effort. As an aside, at this stage most leaders, fearing that such a focus might lose them valuable revenue or performance (in a world in which nobody and no system is perfect) will create a number of special categories for the remaining 80 per cent (not just A, B and C players but A+ etc).

The 1 per cent of people who actively contribute to online communities are the pigs of our story (ie people who will allocate free time and resources to making the community work). If you use that insight against your segmentation you will find that, in fact, roughly 1 per cent of your customers and employees are active participants. Whilst 20 per cent of customers might provide you with 80 per cent of your revenue and 20 per cent of your employees might provide you with 80 per cent of your performance, only 1 per cent of your customers and employees do more than purchase or perform. That 1 per cent define themselves through your product and services. They evangelize and advocate. So should we segment more violently? Is it worth just identifying the 1 per cent and investing in them? Should we conclude that we have to identify the 1 per cent really engaged, who are probably our masters and shapers (or at least our pigs), and discount rather than count our chickens? The answer is a resounding *NO* and has to do with Levchin's insights into transactional involvement versus social engagement.

The 1 per cent rule tells a different story from the Pareto principle. We need to make a distinction between what I call transactional involvement (active economic participation – ie your 20 per cent) and emotional engagement. What we identify through traditional segmentation methods is transactional involvement. We know the identity of the customers who pay us the most or the employees who perform the best. What the 1 per cent rule forces us to do is recognize that transactional involvement is only sustainable through social engagement but, and here is the big news item, social engagement operates completely independently of transactional involvement.

Transactional involvement is easy to chart. You apply your segmentation rules and find it out – you have the data. In the case of online advertising you call it click-through or eyeball. Social engagement works differently. Think about it this way. The reason I chose to live where I do is because of the strong community. We have local newsletters that get posted through my door. We have clubs of all sorts for all ages. We have a festive dinner organized by some residents during the holiday season for those community members who are alone or less fortunate. We have a 'help squad' of volunteers looking out for the weaker members of our community. The place is wonderful and without such an active community I would not have transacted (ie moved in), given the outrageous cost of London property!

But, whilst the community (driven by 1 per cent of residents) is the main reason I transacted, I am not, in any way, actively involved with it. I do not write or distribute the newsletter (yet I love it and look forward to it every month). I do not belong to any of the clubs (yet it's nice to know they are there). I do not help at the dinner or with the help squad (yet I feel proud and reassured by being part of a community that cares).

I matter to the community for the economic contribution I make to it but that's all. I am your typical dependent. So the question in business terms is this – were I to be your employee or customer what would you do with me? Am I in your 80 or 20 per cent? Do you invest in me on the basis of my transaction or do you dismiss me on the basis of my lack of social engagement? It is a complicated picture, but the likelihood is that you would recognize me as valuable (nothing extraordinary there).

Now how about the community itself? How about if I tell you that most of the masters and shapers in my apartment block are in fact on a special rental arrangement negotiated some time ago that generates the least revenue and the greatest costs of any of the properties in the block? Participants are a mix of low rent and high rent payers. What do you do with them? Do you allocate them in your 20 and 80 per cent buckets on the basis of their economic contribution or do you go wider and somehow account for their social engagement (because that's what attracted me to pay)? As this chapter's title suggests it is hard to know who matters most – the people who play or the ones who pay to watch the play.

The truth is that many chickens transact (ie your 20 per cent) because of the social engagement of your participants (ie pigs). The participants (1 per cent) who give rise to the transactional involvement of the dependents, on the other hand, will only socially engage on the basis of the community's total emotional footprint (irrespective of their transactional level)! What it really means is that our traditional models of engagement, built on historical transactional involvement data, only tell half of the story. So let me try to recap in the hope of achieving some clarity.

Organizations currently focus their effort and spend on key employees and customers identified via a process of segmentation. This process relies on historical purchase and performance data to calculate potential transactional involvement (ie who has contributed to our business success and is likely to continue to do so). This misses out the key ingredient of engagement strategies in the age of mass participation – social engagement. Social engagement explains *why* people contribute to success – it is the driver of transactional involvement. The critical insight for leaders is that social engagement is present throughout a community and whilst some employees and customers might not transact, their social engagement is critical to others doing so.

The mistake leaders are likely to make is to apply the logic of segmentation to the new landscape. They will actively try to dislodge rebels and move everyone else up the community ladder (eg dependents to participants etc). This is not only unnecessary but it will destroy the balance of the community and lead to lower transactional involvement. Chickens and pigs are as intertwined and inseparable as chickens and eggs. To get to the heart of engagement we need to ensure we understand the social engagement architecture of our community.

Having understood it we need to actively engage with the community (at every level) to nurture it, as only this will provide satisfactory levels of coordination – what Philip Rosendale referred to as 'self-policing'. As a new world of mass collaboration is upon us, leaders should stay well away from trying to act as architects and town planners attempting to redesign the communal landscape. Instead, their time will be better spent tending the gardens and renovating the houses to make the place attractive for people who want to move in.

The trends indicate that the coordination of activities we have so far achieved through hierarchical means is not efficient and that the means through which we achieve coordination will need to change. There are two insights we can gain from the trends themselves.

The first is that the coercion of individuals towards an organizational cause (however cleverly articulated or positively intended) is not sustainable. Commitment cannot be engineered. The 'Ikeazation' of the economy demands a 'build it and they will come' mindset rather than a 'lie cleverly and they will buy' capability. Communities do indeed self-regulate, even without centralized control. A complex interaction between transactional involvement and social engagement emerges, which no organization can or should try to regulate.

The second is that the very tools used to create the coordination of activities and the engagement of resources have had their legitimacy rooted in the institutional character of the organization. As these institutions cannot survive we will need to find a new set of tools. The trends are changing the way organizations create. The new units of analysis are not organizations (in the sense of structurally organized), but rather companies (as in groups of companions). Does that mean that leadership will be irrelevant? Are we going towards some anarchical, communal days where no one is in charge (with the associated chaos we have all been taught to fear anarchy leads to)? Well, the way we have led might be irrelevant but this is not true of leadership altogether. We are living beyond the days of leadership. See you in the next chapter to talk about 'leadershift'.

The 30 second recap

The demographic and attention trends are a direct threat to the control we rely on today for effective organizations whilst the expertise and democratic trends mean structures are no longer experienced as legitimate.

Mass participation communities do not rely on structures and control for effectiveness. Rather, they rely on roles underwritten by the needs of their participants. These roles can be split between *engaged* participants in the building of the community (which I call masters, shapers and participants) and *involved* participants who depend on the community but are not shaping it (these I call dependents, platform creators and rebels).

Dependents, platform creators and rebels *transact* with organizations on the basis of the *social engagement* of others. Masters, shapers and participants are *socially engaged* because of the *transactional involvement* of others. Future success means building communities that people want to engage with rather than continuing to structure roles and create segments to make them want to transact.

Notes

1   Dow Jonas (2005) Extra!!: Philip Calls the FBI. W-Hats Shit Themselves, *Second Life Herald*, 14 December.
2   *Rosedale discloses FBI griefing probe to Congress* (2008) Second Life News Center, 1 April.
3   Peter DeGrace and Leslie Hulet Stahl (1990) *Wicked Problems, Righteous Solutions: A catalogue of modern software engineering paradigms*, Prentice Hall.
4   Jessi Hempel and Michael V Copeland (2008) Are These Widgets Worth Half a Billion?, *Fortune*, 25 March.
5   Jessi Hempel and Michael V Copeland (2008) 'Are These Widgets Worth Half a Billion?, *Fortune*, 25 March.
6   Ben McConnell, Jackie Huba (2007) *Citizen Marketeers – When People are the Message*, Kaplan Publishing.

7 Leadershift

We like to think of leaders as the embodiment of the community they represent. But the truth is that, when the DEAD trends are removing structured control over resources, we look to leadership to remove our deep-rooted fear of chaos. This fear is best explained by what has come to be known as 'the tragedy of the commons'.[1]

The tragedy of the commons was first explained by Texan ecologist Garrett James Hardin in his 1968 paper of the same name for the journal *Science*. G J Hardin is a controversial figure, not just because he left us with some questionable wisdom such as the now famous and overused saying 'nice guys finish last', but more importantly because of some of the more controversial outcomes of his stance. It is hard to postulate how many of the consequences of his thinking Hardin actually envisaged or defended. It is, however, easy to assert that such things as state-enforced limits on childbearing in the People's Republic of China, rampant privatization of common goods in most of the Western world and the rejection of education as a force for change in pregnancy management are all policies devised as remedies to the problem he first (arguably wrongly) articulated. 'The tragedy of the commons' goes something like this.

Think about a patch of grass – the common – made freely available for all farmers in a village. It belongs to all of them. They all have free access to it for their cattle to graze. Hardin stipulates that because the benefit applies to each farmer (ie each of them has an incentive to put as many of their cattle on the common as possible) but the cost is shared (ie the degradation of the common as a result of grazing will impact all of them equally), the inherent incentive will eventually destroy the common (ie the incentive to get maximum value from the common will eventually destroy its sustainability). That is unless one of two things happens. Either the common structure itself is destroyed (ie the common is broken into smaller fields – effectively privatized – each belonging to one farmer, to remedy the cost-benefit imbalance) or a strong governance structure is introduced that regulates the way the farmers use the common.

Our fear of abuse of common goods runs deep. When we think about open, self-directed communities, we can't help but muster an image of farmers staring, wide-eyed, shaking their heads, at what used to be their green common lying in ruin due to their own stupidity. We can't help but call for Hardin's only two possible remedies – either break up into small private enterprises or employ strong governance through structured control. Our fear of our very own, seemingly uncooperative, human nature is hard to shake off.[2] We want leaders to provide us with direction.

In Hardin's world, the role of leaders is to prevent the outcomes of our own self-interest through control. By being custodians of the governance structures of the organization, they are the decision makers (or at least owners of the decision-making process). They exert their influence on the system through the authority their position gives them. That's why leadership is so critical.

There are a number of issues with the idea of the tragedy when this is applied more broadly. The first is that, unlike a common, creativity is not a finite resource. The problem of the imbalance between limited supply and 'incentivized' over-demand is not a concern that mass collaboration efforts will suffer. Few organizations complain when demand for their products or services increases. But that is only half of the commons tragedy. The second half is much harder for us to dismiss as it underpins most of our fears about communities. This problem is known to economists as the free rider issue.

Free riders are people who abuse a communal system for their own benefit. If you are an economist whose theories are based on the belief that human beings are rational, it makes perfect sense to stipulate that anyone faced with the possibility of getting something for nothing will always try their luck. I remember my school economics teacher pointing out that the fact that street lights were available to all had the unfair consequence that people who evaded taxes would still benefit from them. Endless discussions ensued about how it may be possible for the local government to issue an electronic tag to tax payers that would light up only their passage. I pictured a line of free riders following tax payers around to benefit from their light. I conceived imaginative new schemes tax payers could use to sell light to free riders in order to recoup their tax payments. But as with the proverbial drunk looking for his lost keys under the street lamp, not because he expects them to be there but because that's the only place with enough light for him to see, we may be looking in the wrong place.

For a start there is one simple truth we need to remember – you cannot steal that which is given to you. Let's go back to our chickens and pigs analysis. We know from 'pay or play' that chickens and pigs are as intertwined and inseparable as chickens and eggs. That is to say, pigs are socially involved in the community because they want to benefit the chickens who also form part of this community. We also know that rebels help reinforce community boundaries. So actually in many cases the free riding problem – as an overarching problem likely to destroy a community – disappears, as any free riding activity results in little to no actual cost to the community.

Looking at the tragedy through a communal lens, what we witness are some farmers (shapers and participants) taking their cows home to accommodate the over-grazing of other farmers' cows (dependents and rebels). This is due to the process of communal self-regulation (ie people are not as bad as Hardin wants us to believe).

In fact, real-world research indicates that some people will harvest less during a period of scarcity. This behaviour is a direct result of social involvement encouraged by close ties amongst community members. These are the close ties that enforced privatization of the common good (ie one of Hardin's proposed solutions) actually destroys (privatization, by definition, is the replacement of communal interests by personal ones). When the community is strong, people exercise restraint and exhibit renewed effort to build bonds to protect the community from scarcity. Furthermore, strong social networks are better protected from tragedy than weak ones. So rather than breaking up the commons we need to strengthen the ties between the farmers. The tragedy leads us up the wrong path.

The problem is not one of competition but rather one of trust. We are not as calculatingly rational as Hardin needs us to be for the tragedy to occur. Community acceptance is important to us and exclusion from the community punitive. Imagine what it would do to your reputation if you were the one who started the whole downward spiral. Strong links are psychologically hard to break. The situation we are in has less to do with the 'tragedy of the commons', but rather with the 'trustworthiness of the community'. It is community-derived rules, rather than a governance structure directed by leaders, that provide the incentive for responsible behaviour.

This analysis, however, does not sit well with the governing view of leadership introduced at the start of this chapter, based as it is on the need for control. Mass collaboration underpinned by active, motivated agents and communal self-regulation requires a new modus operandi. On that basis, whilst (to paraphrase Mark Twain's famous quote) 'the report of leadership's death was an exaggeration',[3] the need for its reinvention remains a necessity.

Given the doomsday scenario painted by the tragedy and the fact that our trends are directing us towards organizations where structures and control are no longer possible, how can we possibly have examples of effective organizational behaviour? Indeed, reading about the open self-directed systems that have become the focus of so much business writing, one is struck by the description of groups of individuals coming together for a greater purpose and requiring little by way of external encouragement to do so.

Whilst most people will have heard of Facebook or MySpace in the same way they will have heard of Apple or Microsoft, if asked on the street, most would not be able to name the leaders of the former whilst being able to wax lyrical about Steve Jobs and Bill Gates.[4] But although street recognition might not be that great for Mark Zuckerberg or Tom Anderson[5] according to any study, book or article you read, they alone account for the existence of businesses built in their own image. Much of that, of course, can be accounted for by our very human need to allocate responsibility for any act (good or bad) to one individual rather than a community. But this should not take away from the paradox of self-directed systems – they seemingly rely on the best leaders for their existence, yet they don't actually need any ongoing leadership to exist. We can all recognize that any community to which we belong has at least one person we can identify as a leader. So, how do we account for this paradox, and can today's leaders become tomorrow's or do they need to change?

To answer these questions I need you to think about blenders for a minute. I know that came out of the blue, even maybe as a bit of a shock, but trust me it will lead somewhere. I need to talk to you about the Blentec K-TEC Kitchen Mill – the blender that revolutionized blending. That blender was created in 1975, by Tom Dickson, founder of the K-TEC company. The reason it caused a stir (can a blender cause a stir?) is because that blender was the start of the company's claim that the Blentec blenders are the strongest blenders on the planet. What happened next is what is important to us here.

How do you substantiate a claim that your blenders are the strongest blenders in the world? Simple – you arrange to blend anything others might consider impossible to blend – golf balls, lighters, garden rakes, diamonds. In fact, if you can think of any more items you don't believe can be blended, get on YouTube or visit willitblend.com, suggest your item and Tom Dickson might well try it, record it and post the resulting film on the site for all to see.[6] The films of the experiments have proved so popular that Blentec started selling the DVD. The willitblend campaign became an internet viral marketing sensation with over 30 million viewers to date. So what does this have to do with leadership?

Well, the thing about willitblend is that nobody forced anyone to watch the clips. Its success rested on a band of loyal followers spreading the message and going out of their way to get others to see it (sending links, interrupting conversations to talk about that cool thing they'd seen on the web). The reason they do so comes down to two key elements. In the words of marketing supremo Seth Godin,[7] for anything to go viral it needs to be worth talking about and easy to talk about. By blending ever more outrageous items, Tom Dickson made Blentec worth talking about. By posting the films on YouTube and asking for suggestions, he made it easy to spread. Now, back to leadership.

When no one has to follow and where leadership at first appears to be unnecessary, as is the case with mass collaboration, why do people choose to follow? The answer is the same for leaders as it is for blenders – to be followed, leaders must be worth following and easy to follow. Now, with that in mind, we can solve the mass collaboration leadership paradox. It is easy to see why open self-directed communities might still value leaders. In fact, it is easy to see why any community might crave this kind of leadership. To cut a long story short, whatever words form part of your analysis, you will always return to the same conclusions: leaders are worth following if they make the community stronger. They are easy to follow if, whilst doing this, they make the community and the individuals within it self-sufficient. It is also clear that you do not need to have a special position or form of control to achieve these aims.

What does making a community stronger look like? To function (ie to not fall for the tragedy), any community (or organization) needs certain conditions to be in place. The first is **engagement**. A community needs followers. We decide a community is worth belonging to if it has a point. It needs to exist for something that it can do. This seems rather obvious but, as I pointed out in my book, *The Connected Leader*, many an organization starts life as a purpose in search of assets only to later become an asset in search of a purpose.

Once we have engagement, we need **alignment** of the community to work towards achieving its objectives. If you join a dancing community to play poker you may be disappointed. Alignment without **accountability**, however, is of little value. We need community members to be clear on the nature of their contribution. For them to feel truly accountable for the outcome we need them to maintain their **commitment**.

The way in which we try achieve engagement, alignment, accountability and commitment in an organization today is through control. We try to direct others' behaviours by engineering effective hierarchies (making them as humane as necessary). We use our influencing tactics to get customers to buy and employees to perform. We segment our customer base to identify who really matters and then engineer attraction, engagement and retention strategies. We segment our employee base to identify who really performs and devise attraction, share of mind, expansion and retention strategies. Faced with any narrative our leadership answer is always the same – find, attract, nurture and convince by engineering solutions.

To engage people in our organizational efforts we look to **clarity**. Leaders try to sell a greater purpose (usually one greater than the menial nature of the organizational reality). Forget installing phone lines if you work in a telco – you are making the world a better place by reducing social distance. Forget selling food if you work in a supermarket – you are in fact making the world a better place by helping families send their children to better schools by keeping the price of what they feed them low. And if your product is not as worthy (manufacturing cigarettes for example) you position your organization as a proponent of freedom for the individual to choose how to live his or her life. Any purpose you can think of always comes back to making the world a better place on the basis of the big picture clarity the leader articulates.

To align people towards the purpose you design **plans**. This is how we're going to change the world. You work hard to ensure the plan links the nature of a role (ie sell food) to the purpose of the organization (ie make the world a better place). And you create accountability by defining **roles**. The role is the unit of analysis. 'This is how what you do fits and therefore if you mess up, we can't change the world.' That certainly is more likely to create commitment than 'If your shelf is not stocked properly, we'll miss some sales!' You hope this will engineer commitment but, if it doesn't, you can always turn to the punitive or encouraging nature of the economic incentive (ie **money**).

You may detect a slight sarcastic tone in the above analysis, but I don't mean to dismiss organizational efforts. Many of the leaders I know embark on this road with honesty. They truly believe their effort changes the world and in some cases it might well do. I have nothing against supermarket companies and telcos. Some of my best friends work in these sectors. What I mean to highlight is that these efforts are doomed to failure unless the role we need people to play is vocational. Few schoolchildren claim to want to be accountants or consultants when they grow up and to try to convince adults who ended up in these fields otherwise is something of a waste of time. The situation is complicated further by the DEAD trends.

The demographic trend means that people no longer look to institutions to provide them with the elements that give meaning to their lives. The expertise trend means that we are now faced with an ecosystem of communities, all with their own aims that cannot be aligned under an organization's overall purpose. The attention trend means that any plan you might have is now pitted against a greater, truer purpose. And finally the democratic shift means that your position within that system no longer comes with the built-in ability to do any of the above. The latter is probably the greatest trend. Remember we got here through the recognition that open communities do not need leaders but rather that they crave them. That is to say that they, not some overarching power, identify who these leaders should be.

In a post-DEAD trends world the needs of the community and the focus of its leaders are the same (engagement, alignment, accountability and commitment) as in a pre-trends world. It is the modus operandi of leadership that needs to change.

Mass collaboration describes all that is social, communal and co-creative in our relationship with business. In that way the term embodies the ability to engage in a two-way creative relationship; what Lawrence Lessig, Professor of law at Stanford Law School and founder of its Center for Internet and Society, calls a change from a 'read only' to a 'read-write' culture. To add value, communities look for a new type of leadership that embodies this two-way relationship. If leadership is about pushing forms of engagement onto others, then what I call 'leadershift' is about facilitating a community's engagement need. It is that new 'leadershift' modus operandi that I define as:

> A type of leadership, non-hierarchical in form, that facilitates the collaboration of a self-selected group, of which the leader is an integral part, in the generation of a narrative that builds and sustains a valuable and co-created outcome.

Arguably many of the terms that have come to define leadership in recent years, from authentic to emotionally intelligent via my own connected, seem to embody the idea of encouraging and enabling others to create (most leaders would probably define their role in these terms). However, where 'leadershift' differs from leadership is in its search for a truly dynamic, social and co-created form of leadership. This is leadership that blurs the boundaries between leader and follower and places the importance of culture facilitation over that of strategy articulation as the central focus of its efforts. Let me try to illustrate what I mean by 'leadershift' by calling on one of the world's best-known and most groundbreaking psychologists – Stanley Milgram.

Stanley Milgram became famous because of two groundbreaking experiments. The first, arguably his most famous, having given rise to a CBS film and a Peter Gabriel song, is one of the most famous psychology experiments to date, which has crossed the boundaries of academia to lodge itself into our common consciousness. Conducted at Yale in 1963 it is simply known as 'the Milgram experiment'. Milgram was keen to understand the nature of our obedience to authority. The experiment (the ethics of which were questioned by the American Psychological Association) was inspired by Milgram's observation of the Nazi regime.

Trying to understand how humans can inflict pain and suffering on each other, he made volunteers subject other volunteers to ever higher levels of electric shocks every time they answered a question wrongly in a quiz. What the volunteers who inflicted the pain did not know is that the people receiving the electric shocks were, in fact, in on the experiment and were never subjected to any pain. What Milgram wanted to know is how far people would go if a man wearing the white coat of scientific authority told them the experiment was safe and that he took responsibility for the outcome. The result that shook the world was that 65 per cent of participants continued through the experiment to administer the highest possible deadly 450-volt shock. Whilst many were uncomfortable (questioning the need to go on), no participant, at any stage, refused to administer shocks until they reached the 300-volt level.

The second Milgram experiment, conducted in 1967 while at Harvard, bears the title 'the small-world experiment' and is widely acclaimed as the source of the phenomenon that has come to be known as 'the six degrees of separation'. For his research, Milgram sent packages to 160 random people living in Omaha, Nebraska, asking them to forward the package on to any acquaintance likely to be able to pass it on to someone who eventually could send the package to a named stockbroker from Boston, Massachusetts. Milgram showed that it took six jumps on average for a package to get to the final destination (hence the now well-used claim, and internet viral phenomenon, that we are only six degrees away from anyone else).[8]

So we now know that we are obedient to authority and incredibly well connected – two important things to know for anyone studying organizations. It is, however, two of Milgram's other findings that help us understand the change of emphasis needed in leading in a post-DEAD trends world.

The first is the identification of what Milgram called 'the familiar stranger'. The word stranger may no longer openly carry the connotation imbued in its Latin roots (in Latin the word stranger is the same as the word for enemy) but in many ways we are still uncomfortable in the presence of strangers (hence the familiar warnings to children). What

Milgram identified in his 1972 paper, 'The Familiar Stranger',[9] is how we can develop, under certain circumstances, a kind of obligation towards people we don't even know.

A familiar stranger can be defined as someone you see repeatedly during your daily activities (commuting or shopping for your lunch for example) but with whom you do not interact. What is so interesting about the familiar stranger is that if you change the context, the relationship changes too. For example imagine you found yourself sitting across from the person whom you see every day on your commuter train, but this time in an unfamiliar city on a business trip. My guess (and Milgram's finding) is that you are more likely to strike up a conversation with that person; after all they are a familiar face. The likelihood is that you feel a bond with a person who was only a stranger the day before, albeit a familiar one.

These findings have become critical to our understanding of how social networks function and how the social obligations that underpin their effectiveness come about. To build a strong community with a single co-creation aim, leaders need to be able to maximize opportunities to build familiar stranger bonds inside the community. This is made even clearer in the next Milgram experiment I need you to consider. This time Milgram, a student of social order, focused on that most human of activities – standing in line.[10]

Standing in line (or queuing as we call it in Britain) is one of these activities we might as well learn to enjoy as we will spend on average more time queuing than we do shopping (the fact that most queuing occurs when shopping should help us psychologically to rejoice at our fate). Any of you familiar with this activity will know of the line-jumping phenomenon (usually started by a foreign visitor unfamiliar with the rules of the game). As a Frenchman having immigrated to Britain over 20 years ago, I can vouch for the fact that those of us who are not Anglo-Saxons find it hard to adapt to the orderly way of the line.

Milgram realized early on that the line provides a perfect setting to understand how social order is created, and how it may provide us with some clues as to how that order is maintained. Think Duck on this one. There are queuing rebels the world over. I am sure you're familiar with the situation. You are standing patiently in line, having waited the required 10 minutes for the slow movement towards the cashier who will finally end your wait and make your dreams come true, when out of nowhere comes the hurried queue-jumper. Unfazed by social concerns, this person has decided that the wait is too long and their time too precious, so they do the unthinkable and jump the line. Most of us live with the regret of not having stopped these saboteurs dead in their tracks. We live with the shame of our own weakness.

Travelling around New York, Milgram and his assistants identified 129 queues they would study. The idea was simple. Arriving at a line, they would enter the queue between the third and fourth person, casually apologize for needing to get in that spot and face forward as if nothing had happened. They would only abandon the queue if challenged or after one minute had elapsed. Now, here is the good news. To the apparently weak out there, let me tell you that we are not alone. Most of the time no one did anything to challenge the intruders. Only on 10 per cent of the occasions did anyone eject the queue-jumpers. In fact, only on 50 per cent of the occasions did anyone do anything resembling a challenge (cast a dirty look, exchange comments with each other, or comment directly to the line-jumper).

Next, Milgram probed deeper into our queuing habits by changing a couple of variables. First he decided to try to double the number of intruders. When he did so the rate of interventions rocketed to over 90 per cent of the time. The second variation was to make the line-jumper stand in front of one of Milgram's colleagues, in effect buffering the jumper against the legitimate queue. When this happened, the number of objections decreased to just five per cent.

So what was going on here? That we are slow to intervene comes as no surprise to most of us but why do we appear so scared to intervene? Here is where Milgram's findings become interesting. While we might assume that fear is our prime concern (after all, continual reports of low urban security must play a part), there are other factors that are much more powerful.

First, Milgram suggests that the fact that we are in line makes social order weak. It is easy to see how, facing each other's backs, we have few opportunities to build the social ties necessary to provide an effective social coalition. There are of course elements of self-interest in our keeping quiet. If we are to intervene, maybe driving the queue-jumper out, we may lose our hard-fought place in the queue.

But more importantly, we are prepared to accept some social deviation as this may be the best way to protect the communal rule. If we were to argue against all disruption, chaos would ensue, so it is in our interest to accept and make the deviant a member of our queue (hoping that once they have joined they'll share our sense of purpose) rather than allow social order to stop altogether. Acceptance of a queue-jumper means this individual gains an interest in the queue and the queue becomes stronger. When deviance becomes too strong (eg we have five line-jumpers instead of one) then we are much more likely to intervene.

There is no need to regulate the queue. It will work as long as the social ties that form it are strong enough. In a social structure, contrary to our assumption when faced with the tragedy of the commons, it is not regulation we need but rather social obligation. Milgram tells us that as long as we can encourage social ties, we are much more likely to have order.

'Leadershift' is about capitalizing on familiar strangers by reinforcing the social ties that bind us. I have a picture on my desk designed to remind me of the nature of the change effort from leadership to 'leadershift'. On it is that much overused stock photo of the gold-fish jumping from a small bowl to a bigger one. That goldfish is a metaphor for leadership. As the world becomes confusing, leaders focus on getting better at what they do. They want to do more of the same in a better and more effective way. They aim to increase their impact – moving from the small to the big bowl. That's fine, except that in my picture, the two bowls stand on a beach with the ocean in the background.

This helps to remind me that whilst the goldfish, for good reasons, may feel more comfortable and satisfied in its bigger bowl, it could have ensured a brighter future by making the jump from the small bowl to the ocean rather than just to a bigger bowl. The task at hand is not to change or refine the style of leadership we use to be effective. Rather it is about changing our focus to see and embrace the opportunities offered by a new environment. This is the opportunity 'leadershift' offers.

This new focus is best illustrated by the kind of titles leaders in open systems have been using to describe what they do. Few leaders in organizations today, even if they wish they could, would ever openly embrace the 'Benevolent Dictator' or 'Benign Dictator' title most of Wikipedia gives to its founder Jimmy Wales, or the one of 'the most trusted party (TMTP)' Linus Torvald of Linux has been given, or the other examples such as 'constitutional monarch', '*Eminence Grise*' or '*Deus ex Machina*' that have been suggested in communities throughout the world. These kinds of autocratic titles would be rejected by most organizations as not representative of the visionary and democratic behaviours they wish their leaders to display. Yet, if you are called to facilitate the functioning of the community by shaping its culture, this is exactly what you are called upon to do.

In this context, the symbolic figure helps provide a shared identity, a sense of values and a coherent message. The leader becomes a facilitator rather than a director. The legitimacy of prophetic leaders, even in times of seismic change, is only rooted in their ability to facilitate the creation of cultural ties. Whilst maybe less dramatic than the personal heroics we like to witness, the role of the leader as a single agent in a system of many is more potent, as it is the resulting culmination of communal interactions that leads to the definition of a new form of engaged coordination.

'Leadershift' actions and behaviours are only legitimate in so far as they are mandated by the community itself. To make a call because no one else can make it is only directive if the community never recognized you as being able to make that call. When the community asks you to arbitrate its decisions, a directive style becomes a helpful style. The chickens are happy for pigs to make decisions because this is the very role they have allocated to them.

The difference between leadership and 'leadershift' rests in the focus of the leaders as well as the source of their legitimacy. In 'leadershift', reputation rather than position makes the leader. What creates a reputation is the commitment the leader has shown to the community rather than the effectiveness by which they have made it work for their benefit. That kind of power is interdependent. The leader is only as strong as the community is and the community becomes stronger through the actions of its leaders. The difference between current organizational positional power and this communal, social power is that both parties need to agree and have the ability to review the contract. When Larry Sanger, co-founder of Wikipedia,[11] resigned, many saw this as a direct result of his loss of legitimacy in the community through his autocratic actions that were not mandated by the community.

Of course, much of Wales's and Torvald's legitimacy rests on their reputations as founders of their respective communities. If you start a movement it is easy to see why the community would defer to you when it is stuck in its decision making. However, whilst founders might have an inbuilt reputation they also have the disadvantage of seeing their creation take on a life of its own. Jimmy Wales himself, in his 2005 TED presentation, stresses that he can only play this role as long as the community decides he is the best one to play it.[12]

The emergent nature of 'leadershift' is what differentiates it from its forebear. The source of your power as a leader is the community. It alone gives legitimacy to the role it is asking you to play. That role is to make the community stronger. When you use your power for any other purpose, or when the community feels that you have not added the value it expected, it will withdraw that support. Under current organizational structures, you may well keep your role and a semblance of power afforded by the structure; however, that power is invisible to the community. The community places its trust in a group of individuals (masters, shapers and participants) that it believes will, through role modelling, arbitration and attention, help it shape its culture. That trust is regularly reviewed to ensure it is well allocated. In these instances, creating engagement as well as ensuring resource alignment, accountability and commitment requires a focus

Table 7.1 Shifts from leadership to leadershift

Leadership Inputs	Organizational Outputs	Leadershift Inputs
clarity	engagement	simplicity
plans	alignment	narratives
roles	accountability	tasks
money	commitment	love

on augmenting the existing communal characteristics rather than injecting a new focus.

The reason this book is called *Leadershift* rather than *Organizationshift* and has 'reinventing leadership' rather than 'reconstructing organizations' as its subtitle is because I firmly believe (and intend to show) that only a series of shifts in leaders' mindsets will help us meet the challenges of our times. The fact that some of our current organizational tools (such as roles) might still be legitimate constructs as we move forward does not mean that they are sufficient to engage people in an age of mass collaboration. Indeed I hope, as we move through this journey together, that, like me, you will become convinced that it is only by shifting our mindset that we will be able to reinvent organizations able to withstand ambient turbulence.

It is for these reasons that the following chapters look at the practices that make a leader's role worthwhile, in demand and sustainable. By moving away from clarity, plans, roles and money and focusing instead on simplicity, narratives, tasks and love (yes, I know, that may not be to everybody's taste, but trust me on this one), leaders can help the community release its value and function at its best. Mass collaboration wants 'leadershift' even if it doesn't need leadership. In fact, let's start our exploration by hanging out with Jimmy Wales a little while longer.

The 30 second recap

Not only do the trends eradicate the effectiveness of structures in gaining control over resources, they also force us to question the need for leadership. The presence of a leader in communities is not to govern, in order to mitigate for a perceived lack of trust, but rather to help the community construct the social norms and ties that bind it to a common effort. I have come to call this 'leadershift' and to define it as follows:

A type of leadership, non-hierarchical in form, that facilitates the collaboration of a self-selected group, of which the leader is an integral part, in the generation of a narrative that builds and sustains a valuable and co-created outcome.

In this context leaders build their legitimacy through their reputation in being able to provide the community with the tools it needs, without any imposition other than that called for by the community itself.

Notes

1　Garrett Hardin (1968) The tragedy of the commons, *Science*, **162**, pp 1243–48.
2　For further discussions and insights on the economic impact of 'The tragedy of the commons' you may want to turn to one of the first in-depth studies of the open source movement. In his book *The Cathedral and the Bazaar* (O'Reilly, 1999), Eric S Raymond takes a deeper look at the economics of the tragedy as applied to open source than it is possible or appropriate to cover here. Raymond is one of the founding fathers of the open source movement and this book is acknowledged by most as being 'the shot that resonated around the world' and started a global movement.
3　There exist many versions of this quote using different words but all conveying the same meaning. I have settled for what appears to be the official version as written in a note from Mark Twain to the *New York Journal* in May 1897.
4　OK so you did know the names, but you're not your average person in the street now are you? For a start you're reading this book.
5　Maybe as a reminder that things are never as straightforward as they seem in the world of creation, debates are always going on (with threatened lawsuits to boot) about who the real founders are of many

web and non-web businesses. I have named Mark and Tom here as they are the two people most often recognized as the founders of Facebook and MySpace.

6 Just so you know, to date Chuck Norris is the only thing that has proved too strong for the blender. Nobody can blend Chuck Norris. Check it out at willitblend.com.

7 Seth Godin (2007) *Meatball Sundae – How New Marketing is Transforming the Business World*, Piatkus.

8 There have been reviews of the claim since and other scientists have questioned Milgram's findings.

9 Stanley Milgram (1972) The familiar stranger: An aspect of urban anonymity, *Division 8 Newsletter*.

10 Stanley Milgram, Hilary J Liberty, Raymond Toledo and Joyce Wackenhut (1986) Response to intrusion into waiting lines, *Journal of Personality and Social Psychology*, **51** (4), pp 683–89.

11 There is a lot of debate about the nature of the role Larry Sanger played in creating Wikipedia, most of which is played out in Jimmy and Larry's respective entries on the site. My aim is not to fuel this debate but to report concerns others have articulated.

12 Jimmy Wales (2005) *Jimmy Wales: How a ragtag band created Wikipedia*, TED talk, Global TED Conference [Online] www.TED.com.

8 Shift 1 – from clarity to simplicity

Before we can make any community stronger and therefore justify our existence as leaders, we need to somehow make sure there is a community! The need to engage other people must be our starting point. However, something may not be quite as we would like it. The whole point of engagement is that people should feel comfortable with the work they do and the way they do it. That, however, is not how work feels these days for leaders and followers alike.

The first symptom of the unease created by the DEAD trends is complexity. Nothing confirms the change we are facing more than our recent awakening to the fact that organizations have become complex to the point of distraction if not destruction. In the face of this complexity, leaders renew their efforts at providing even more clarity. But these efforts are largely wasted. Complexity is the symptom of a deep condition for which clarity is not a cure. Let's get back to Jimmy Wales to gain some insights into what might be happening, why it matters and what we can do about it.

Jimmy Donal 'Jimbo' Wales is hardly someone you would call the poster child of the so-called 'web 2.0' revolution,[1] that new wave of internet ventures trumpeting creativity and collaboration as their core offering. For a start, his birth in 1966 makes him older than the 16- to 20-year-olds most of us picture as the vanguards of the internet revolution. And whilst he is not averse to publicity, controversy and public appearances, his more philosophical musings on the status of communal engagement, along with his self-description as 'objectivist to the core', make him an unlikely contender for the coolest entrepreneur award so many journalists are keen to bestow on much of Silicon Valley's population.[2] But even if Jimbo doesn't fully represent our stereotype, it's worth remembering that in 2006, as the co-creator of the world's largest encyclopaedia, he was named one of 'the world's most influential people' by *Time* magazine. Whilst he may not be the father of so-called 'web 2.0'[3] per se, being the founder of Wikipedia makes him at the very least the man responsible for making it popular.

Wikipedia began life as a project for Nupedia. Despite being online, Nupedia was similar to Encyclopaedia Britannica or its DVD-based 'Encarta' competitor. It was written and edited by experts and followed the strict peer review process encyclopaedias have adopted since the 18th-century days of Diderot's and d'Alembert's *Encyclopédie*. The main difference between Nupedia and others was its price. Nupedia was free, both in terms of price and content, operating as it did under an Open Content Licence.

Jimmy Wales was CEO of Bomis Inc, the company behind Nupedia, and Larry Sanger its editor-in-chief. Taking his lead from Wales's dream of creating an encyclopaedia all could contribute to, Sanger suggested they use the nascent wiki technology. Wikis are web pages designed in such a way that anyone who can access them over the internet can edit them. Sanger understood that this would open Nupedia up to thousands if not millions of new contributors and editors. Wikis would speed up Nupedia's development whilst transforming it into the true collaborative effort Wales dreamed of. As a result of this new technology, Wikipedia was born in earnest on 15 January 2001.

To say Wikipedia had few rules would be an understatement. It had only the one, carried over from the Nupedia days. The fact that that rule is the 'neutral point of view' rule (ie we do not take sides in what is and isn't worth publishing) is almost better described as a 'no rules' rule.

What makes Wikipedia so different, however, is not just its minimal regulatory framework – rare for any organization – but, more importantly, its submission policy. Unlike other encyclopaedias, it has no peer review process. Changes to any articles can be made by anyone at any time – and they are (research conducted by computer science student Virgil Griffith traced the source of millions of changes to corporations and government agencies eager to 'manage' their image). This open policy accounted for Wikipedia's unprecedented growth. By the end of its first year in existence, it counted 20,000 articles and 18 language editions. A year later that had grown to 26 languages and by its third birthday it counted 161. By 9 September 2007 its English edition passed the significant 2 million article mark, making what many decry as an amateur venture the world's largest encyclopaedia.

Much has been written about Wikipedia's reliability and much of this is underpinned by the cynicism one expects of a world that views expertise as the preserve of the few. Whilst it is true that it can carry errors, the difference between Wikipedia and Encyclopaedia Britannica is actually fairly small.[4] Critics also choose to conveniently forget that, unlike any other encyclopaedia, Wikipedia is instantly editable and continuously updated (the point was well made when, at a conference, a page was updated and a mistake erased as the moderator was pointing it out to Jimbo). Despite its exaggerated potential flaws, Wikipedia's editorial policy has had two major benefits.

One is that it has encouraged many to contribute, tapping into pockets of knowledge previously unexplored. This has ensured that knowledge is richer and free from censure (a fact supported by the eagerness of some regimes, like the Chinese government, to block access to some parts of the site they consider to be politically inappropriate).

The second is that this lack of censure and editorial decision-making has led to multiple entries on topics of interest normally outside the realm of academic interest. A quick search for Barbie in any encyclopaedia is likely to yield articles on Klaus Barbie, the Gestapo officer arrested and tried in France. In Wikipedia, you would have to type his first and second name to get to the 1,000 or so words devoted to him, as searching for Barbie alone would have taken you to some of the 4,000 words written about the doll cherished by generations of little girls. And this last point is the one I wanted to make – not through any particular attachment to the plastic (in every sense of the word) blonde, but rather because it will help us to understand how a community's growth increases its complexity. In fact, let's stick with Jimbo and the Wikipedians for a little while longer.

The Wikipedia community is a typical example of the 'pay or play' topography of social engagement. It is no surprise that Jimbo is known to embrace the 1 per cent rule. He has argued that, much like in any other organization, 'a dedicated group of a few hundred volunteers' is responsible for much of Wikipedia's functioning.[5] Not everybody contributes to the same extent and some people never contribute at all, preferring instead to use the encyclopaedia as a resource. We have a social engagement structure with both pigs and chickens.

Let's start with the pigs.[6] There are two types of people who contribute to Wikipedia – registered and non-registered. Anyone can sign on but not everybody does. Registered members are known to the community. Together these contributors represent the pigs. In our topology we looked at masters and shapers; in Wikipedia these registered members split into three levels of editors. Editors are the caretakers of the community. Their task is to edit articles that have an impact community-wide (difficult disputed issues), as well as banning rebels (yes, Wikipedia has a few Ducks too) from using vandalism editing (making rude comments rather than adding facts for example).

The editor levels start with 'administrator'. Administrators are the largest group (the English edition of Wikipedia has about 1,500 of them). They are sometimes referred to as 'Privileged Users' as they have the ability to delete pages, stop articles from being edited (for fear of vandalism for example – as is common with contentious subjects such as the George W Bush page) and lock articles in cases of editorial dispute.

Wikipedia uses two types of protection for certain articles. Some are semi-protected, which means they can only be edited by registered users who have logged in and been registered for more than four days. They carry the following warning: 'Editing of this article by unregistered or newly registered users is currently disabled'. This ensures that casual browsers cannot leave a graffiti-style edit on something they don't like. Articles in this category have ranged from Sex to Genetic Engineering. The more draconian use of locking a page for protection is full protection. In this case the protected page can only be edited by administrators. Full protection is often used to stop what has been called an 'edit war', where two sides take it in turn to make their opposing views known by editing the page. This is why such pages often carry the warning: 'This page is currently protected from editing until disputes have been resolved'. This status is often reserved for highly contentious and politically loaded pages such as the entry on the 11 September 2001 attacks.

Despite this ability to lock pages, however, administrators do not have any decision-making privileges. They cannot decide on the outcome of a dispute. They owe their position to their credibility (which comes mainly from devotion to the cause). After administrator, the role of editor can move up to 'steward' and eventually 'bureaucrat' (not a title many people would fight for in business today). Together, they are our 1 per cent. That doesn't mean that they write the whole encyclopaedia themselves. On the contrary, like all masters and shapers, they rely on an army of participants who contribute to the cause.

Unregistered users also contribute entries. Their contribution to the community is important by virtue of its size (it is by far the most prolific source of entry) and its quality (it carries equal value). A group of researchers from Dartmouth College in Hanover, NH, found in a 2007 study that non-registered contributors to Wikipedia are as reliable a source of knowledge as registered members. The researchers called them 'Good Samaritans'. We can call them participants. They participate in the growth of the community.[7] They are socially engaged. Their contribution is the equivalent of injecting new genes into a gene pool; it increases the likelihood of the knowledge on Wikipedia being free from bias. Together, masters, shapers and participants actively build the community.

But as well as the pigs who show their commitment, there are Wikipedian chickens who are involved. These are the millions of dependents who have come to rely on Wikipedia as a source of knowledge. But whilst dramas can be played out and knowledge can be disputed, the encyclopaedia's 'neutral point of view' rule ensures Wikipedia remains a serious effort at cataloguing knowledge. Finally, the Wikipedia Foundation can be seen as the platform creator in the same way as Linden Lab created the Second Life platform. It has an all-important role to play in the existence of the encyclopaedia but, in reality and in status, it is still a chicken.

The main acid test for the value of an encyclopaedia is the reliability of the knowledge it contains. So whilst pigs do not have to be authorities in their field, an intricate system of verifiable and published sources is used to determine the accuracy and the value of contributions. Of course some masters and shapers are experts in a subject area, but the main source of expertise is the community. However, as in all fast-growing communities, debates are rife inside Wikipedia about how to best cope with that growth. And this is where we get back to Barbie. There is a debate raging in Wikipedia that goes right to the heart of the engagement issue and, you've guessed it, Barbie is partly responsible.[8] Some argue that it is that balance of credibility through consensus rather than credentials that encourages the richness of the community and warrants the 'anti-elitism' label Wikipedia has often received, whilst others see it as a problem. The participants in this debate can be polarized into two camps – 'inclusionists' versus 'deletionists'.

In the inclusionists' corner sits the belief that Wikipedia should never be limited. Inclusionists argue that given its web rather than paper format, Wikipedia's growth is unlimited. So what if the community writes more about Barbie the doll than they do about Barbie the Nazi?

In time, hopefully the Nazi article can grow through contributions and in any case the space taken up by the doll doesn't in any way impair the growth of further investigations into the Nazi regime. It's not even as though 'less worthy' articles make it hard for dependents to find what they are looking for, given that the way to access content is via a pretty smart search facility.

In fact, the more people are drawn to contribute, regardless of the 'worthiness' of their chosen topic, the more the word is likely to spread that everyone is welcomed, and in time experts will be drawn to the community too. Their only rule is that the article must show credibility under the established processes (for example if your topic of choice only has a few Google entries it is unlikely to be included).

In the deletionists' corner sits the strong sense that the more topics of debatable value are included (they cite such entries as side characters from the Pokémon cartoon or the Heroes TV series as examples), the more dependents will see Wikipedia as a source of fun rather than knowledge. They are worried that the brand is at risk of losing its value. In a deletionist world, Wikipedia would exert more control over what it publishes. Feel free to have a few key Pokémon characters covered (and even some words about Barbie) but work hard to ensure Klaus gets a serious mention. The more trivial articles are included, they argue, the more participants will see Wikipedia as their chance to write about their obscure pet projects.

What this debate raises, however, is not just what the engaged community might do, but rather how you engage the community in the first place. What both camps agree on is that defining what is worthy is not easy. Is it really the case that Klaus Barbie is more important than the Barbie doll? As silly as it may seem at first glance, they have both profoundly impacted society's image of itself.

Every day, administrators are making decisions about whether to include something or not. The way decisions are made is complex. Normally this works through a panel. Any new addition is flagged. If administrators feel this doesn't meet the notability criteria (it is well documented and passes the Google test) they can nominate the entry for deletion. There are, of course, different levels of deletion demands! When an article is flagged for deletion, an appeal can be made and a complex bartering process (consisting of back and forth information demands) starts. If it all goes wrong and administrators are deadlocked, they can go to an Arbitration Committee, requesting a final call.

The problem for anyone other than the most ardent of masters and shapers is that the whole process is not only difficult to understand but the acronyms and precedents used are impossible to get your head around if you want to put up a worthy defence. As a result, the community finds itself deadlocked. An inward-looking army of hacks who have learnt to enjoy the fight rather than the overall vision risks replacing a thriving community of ideas. As it becomes ever more complex, the community could split. Already, competing projects have been put in place, including the entry of almighty Google into the fray with 'Knol', its own version of Wikipedia. Alternatively, it might disintegrate into a side project or even, gasp of horror, a normal encyclopaedia.

Whatever happens to Jimbo and his Wikipedia, it seems that as it grows and complexity takes hold, Wikipedia, like many communities before it, loses engagement. Even if it can be argued that lower contribution levels might be an indication of Wikipedia's maturity (ie it has written most of what can be written), the need to edit and update is still a task one would expect a large number of people would undertake. Complexity is the symptom of a world that no longer makes sense and as it grows, engagement falters. My friends at Royal Philips Electronics identified that issue loud and clear when they looked at how they could best position their products in an ever-changing marketplace.

To understand their customers they conducted a large-scale piece of research into society's needs. It spanned thousands of people across seven countries. The biggest issue they identified was not only clear but also carried an unprecedented sense of urgency. Andrea Ragnetti, Philips's Chief Marketing Officer, puts it this way: 'Almost immediately, we hit on the notion of complexity and its relationship to human beings'.[9] Philips's leaders were not only tapping into the zeitgeist in order to demonstrate some marketing savvy, they were also witnessing a call resonating across the world. Everywhere they went, everyone they spoke to, everything they saw always brought them back to one point – the world is at risk of becoming too complex for us to engage with it.

Let's try to deconstruct what's going on. We relate to things on the basis of coherence. We look at how something fits with what we are trying to achieve. For example, we like our car because it gets us from A to B, or we like our new MP3 player because it breaks the monotony of our day by helping us listen to music while we are on the go. That function gives the overall object a coherence.

Now think about what happens when the battery in either your car or your MP3 packs up. When that happens, things no longer make sense. You suddenly realize that what had coherence is rather more complicated than at first thought. Your car is no longer a car but a pile of separate parts that are quite complex and no longer operate in harmony. The MP3 player is no longer a software-driven clean customer experience but a pile of plastic and metal bits glued together that refuse to function as one. When one part stops functioning, the entire system lacks coherence.

Social network theorists (ie people who study how networks form and stay together) call our ability to make sense of objects as one cohesive whole rather than a complicated number of parts 'punctualization'. They stipulate that it results from numerous, repeated interactions in the systems. The more you use your MP3 player and discuss it with others, the more likely it is that 'punctualization' will happen and the MP3 player will become a tool that brightens your day.

'Depunctualization' occurs when parts of the network are no longer functioning in line with the whole (ie the battery dies). Depunctualization causes stress. It is the stress caused by depunctualization that we experience as complexity (call breakdown company, get car to garage, diagnose fault, order part, repair engine…). We know that a breakdown is not an insurmountable occurrence but that doesn't stop us feeling despair. The system might be straightforward to fix but even if we can comprehend that stress intellectually, it is no less difficult to deal with it emotionally. It is that depunctualization-induced stress that makes us so reluctant and incompetent in the face of complexity.

I can understand my car as an object that helps me travel as long as I don't have to understand it as multiple pieces refusing to start on a cold morning. The lesson Philips drew from their analysis was that, whilst products can be technologically complex, they do not have to be complicated. The distinction is more than mere semantics. The opposite of complex is independent. The opposite of complicated, on the other hand, is simple. A complex product is one that is coherent with parts that are interdependent. A simple, complex product is one that makes sense. It is a product that, despite its engineering complexity, is coherent and intuitive. Only that product can secure our engagement.

That which is true of objects like cars is also true of how we relate to the world at large. The increase in complexity (interdependence) in our world is making it more difficult for us to comprehend. As we experience depunctualization in our local conditions as a result of actions in global settings, stress increases.

That which is true of the world at large is also true of the world of work. As we experience complexity inside our organizations, leaders seek to deliver clarity by removing obstacles (ie simplification). This reasoning appears, at first, faultless. If you remove obstacles, you end up with something simple to understand, easy to cope with and indeed straightforward to engage with. Leaders hope that clarity will remove the stress we experience when facing ambiguous 'depunctualized' situations.

But let's be really clear, there is no real physiological human need for clarity. Clarity is not the source of engagement. The more we experience DEAD trends-induced complexity in our organizations, the more we seem to yearn for simpler times. But is this really what we are after? In our car example, simpler times meant horses and carts and few of us would really like to go back to those times. The problem isn't some aversion to change and progress – we do like our cars and many of us look to upgrade to ever more advanced ones. But we want our cars to make sense and feel simple.

The answer is not clarity but rather what Philips have called 'sense and simplicity'. 'Sense and simplicity' comes as a result of understanding that disengagement is the direct result of depunctualization. What we require as a first step towards engagement, therefore, is not so much clarity as it is coherence, which we gain primarily through simplicity. That is to say that what the community at Wikipedia is expressing by decreasing contribution is not that they need more clarity about the mission of Wikipedia, but rather that they need a simpler way to engage with it. There are two elements to simplicity – simplification and coherence.

Simplification is what most of us have come to describe when we talk about clarity. Simplification is easy for most organizations versed in the art of engineering to understand and practise. Many of the efforts to tackle complexity in recent years have been squarely in the simplification camp. We trust that by simplifying processes, products, reporting lines and channels we will deliver more clarity. Given that most organizations still carry far too many legacy structures and processes that are no longer useful, these efforts have paid off.

In our Wikipedia example, the leadership provided by Jimmy Wales plays a useful simplification role. We know from our last chapter that any attempt at regulating the community would be counterproductive. However, we can imagine Jimmy helping the community reflect on its processes. He could challenge some of the jargon being used. His credibility gives him sufficient power to force a collective reflection on the need for simplification. In many ways as the debate is raging, his contribution as moderator would help channel the community's energy towards a simplified modus operandi, which in turn would encourage further contribution. After all, Wikipedia itself has a 'Simple English Edition', showing that not only does it understand the need for simplification but it also knows what to do with it.

However, simplification and the search for efficient perfection is only one part of the clarity story. A leader must learn to distinguish between what matters and what doesn't to the engagement of a community. Our simplification reflexes have become so sharp that, in our search for efficiency, we risk eradicating some important elements of the community's strength. In the same way as we are quick to reject low-profitability customers and non-performing employees (as we saw in Chapter 6), we are prone to eradicate important routines.

In fact, it turns out that much of the language used by Wikipedians in their debates helps the community define itself. As a result eradicating it may help in one way but hinder in another. The simplification game is not easy. There is no easy answer to the problem other than a constant vigilance on the part of the leader to reflect on what helps or hinders engagement. That is why leadership is a full-time job and it is also why the reflection must be community-wide rather than leader-centric.

On its own, simplification is a futile exercise. Forget cars and MP3s and look at your mobile phone. Mobile telecommunication technology has come a long way in a relatively short time. In fact, crystal clear calls can now be made from one mobile device to another. For years, engineers worked on the best possible way of tackling the ambient noise that could interfere with your call. Like with most things human beings set their minds and resources to, the holy grail of clear calls was eventually reached.

Calls could finally be made with all white noise filtered out. The result was not the one expected, however. The introduction of the technology led to more negative feedback from users than any previously received as a result of white noise. The clarity we seek in our calls is no different from the clarity we seek more broadly. Yes the calls had become perfect and as simple as they could ever be, but callers were lost.

At the end of every sentence, in the absence of any noise before the other person's reply, callers were forced to ask 'Are you still there?' as they thought the absence of white noise meant the line had gone dead. After one mobile phone exchange when both parties have to ask 'Are you still there?' about 15 times, you start to yearn for imperfection. Give us back white noise. And so they did. Engineers had to construct a way of pumping back white noise into conversations through a device analysing the ambient noise on the line and replaying a digital version of it. That's why if you have ever been put on hold when on your mobile phone the background music played never comes out right (it is punctuated with strange white noise), as the system does not quite know what to make of music as a white noise and therefore computes the playback badly (although arguably much of the hold music in use in the world is not far removed from noise).

So, back to organizations. Our ability to get rid of the white noise doesn't actually increase simplicity, and nor for that matter does it create sustainable engagement. We have all witnessed how changes in processes and structure (even if as a result these are becoming simpler) tend to decrease, rather than increase, levels of understanding. We have all seen employees trying to figure out who and what matters once a new structure is announced. So whilst the simplification process is a worthwhile thing to do, it is not the only thing that matters to increasing engagement. What we ignore when we put our focus solely on simplification is the interplay between simplification and our second element of simplicity – coherence. The white noise in our phone example actually made sense to people. It was an integral part of the call experience rather than a complicated add-on.

We can apply the same thinking to Wikipedia. Whilst simplifying the submission process might help resolve some of the issues, it will not create long-term engagement without coherence. Indeed, the very essence of Wikipedia is the richness of the debate that accompanies submission. That debate provides the search for knowledge many seek. Debate, in and of itself, is not inefficient if it helps you achieve the purpose in a richer way than an authoritarian decree would. In the case of a community such as Wikipedia it is in fact essential to the survival of the community. With a group of reviewers and an editorial board, Wikipedia as a community no longer makes sense; it becomes like any other encyclopaedia. The community is both a network and a single entity that stands for something. If simplification addresses the need for the network to be more efficient, coherence ensures communal cohesion.

The role of the leader must be to deploy strategies that can help bring different elements together to build a coherent whole. The leader becomes a primary agent in helping the community stage discussions on what it stands for. The role of leadership is to help communities articulate the problem they are looking to solve. Leaders become representations (as well as representatives) of their communities. It is their role to establish themselves as the 'obligatory passage point' (as agent network theorists call them) between the community and its actors.

In the case of Jimbo, this takes the form of building his credibility and the community at the same time. Leaders spread the word internally and externally, projecting an image of the community they aim to foster, thus helping the community participate in a discussion on its value. Through their actions, they provide a steady beat against which the community can improvise. By keeping a consistent message that reinforces a vision of the community's value, leaders help a community find its own rhythm.

This may seem somewhat abstract for a business book so let me try to make it practical. At its core, any organization (whether open or closed) has a beat. It may be a routine (we always meet on a Friday) or a calendar (we do weekly updates, monthly calls, quarterly results and yearly reviews). Or it may be less obvious but no less rhythmic than that (we always argue about who should buy coffee when we run out). Whatever they are, these instances are sources of rhythm the leader can draw on to become the central focus of communal discussions. They establish routines and rituals that make things coherent and therefore easier to engage with.

In the midst of the uncertainty created by turbulence, this idea of beat ensures we can still operate by balancing the uncertain with the known. We can find the beat of our business by looking at the relationships we have with our team (ie anyone who contributes to the delivery of our objective rather than the people who directly report to us). The best way to map out the nature of that community is by taking the chicken and pig nomenclature (remember from Chapter 6). We need to understand the nature of the relationships between the different actors. Where do they meet? What do they talk about? Is it for information, for discussion, for decision-making? Answering all of these questions will help us focus on the events that mark our communal life.

My guess is that most of these artefacts of our culture are present in your business and you may even follow them instinctively. They have almost become less important (the weekly meeting is probably the first thing to go when a customer calls in tough times). Yet, this beat is as important as the foundations in your house. You don't think about them. You probably would rather invest in a new interior decor. But trust me, when they go, you'll know.

Engagement is fragile. As illustrated by the Wikipedia example, an open system is not intrinsically coherent either. Coherence needs to be created through a number of activities best conducted by a leader who, as shown in the previous chapter, provides a voice and identity for the community. I started this chapter by pointing out that we are aiming to get rid of stress rather than searching for clarity. Routines provide us with a renewed sense of control through coherence. This beat of the organization provides us with psychological health and well-being. Let me close this chapter with an example of simplicity at work.

As with, I suspect, most other writers, coffee is currently playing an important role in my ability to meet publishing deadlines. Whilst writing this book I came across the current marketing campaign run by the almighty Starbucks in the UK. It is a strange choice for a company that has been criticized for having too complex a product range to display posters proudly advertising its 87,000 drink combinations. Indeed trend watchers, spurred on by the Philips research, might feel that at a time of unprecedented complexity, Starbucks would do well to restrict its product range by simplifying it.[10]

But once we know that simplification is only part of the simplicity story (arguably less than half of it), the campaign seems to make sense. What the Starbucks' posters are declaring, by stressing the combinations and the provenance of the coffee, is that you can get whatever you want but one thing you can be sure of is that it will be a consistently high-quality, ethically produced drink. That's coherence. In this instance, 87,000 is the most efficient point of simplification to make that claim. It is that claim, based on simplicity, that ensures we engage with the brand.

The only reason we are prepared to go repeatedly out of our way to make sure we can get combination 63,756 of the 87,000 choices we have is because the promise Starbucks makes through its simplicity fits the way we want to see ourselves. We build our lives by aligning to a number of networks that help us write our stories. It is these stories that help us engage with one network over another, and so it is with any organization.

'Leadershift' in Starbucks is not about a restricted view of clarity (we will open or close so many branches) or an inflated view of its own purpose (we will save the world through serving coffee). It is simply about constantly searching for the occasions when the community can input to its future direction.

Of course, what is important to us, as leaders, is not only that people choose our network to invest their time, money and efforts, but that they do so in a way that is beneficial to the organization. We call it alignment. Without it we fear that, instead of getting people involved in a concerted co-creation effort focused in one direction, we may end up with a multitude of unfocused, wasted enthusiasm. In organizations today we use plans to achieve alignment. But in the turbulent world brought about by our trends, plans become too quickly redundant. Leadershift needs us to look for something different. This is where we are going next and we have Granny Sue as our guide.

The 30 second recap

Complexity is not a critical business issue. The stress that it puts on us is. Clarity does nothing to remove that stress. The key to effective engagement is simplicity. Simplicity is about realigning participants' intellectual and emotional outlooks. It is a combination of two elements.

First comes simplification, which plays an important role in eliminating legacy processes and systems that no longer add value.

The second element is coherence. Coherence is the ability to highlight the interdependence of a system (eg a car is a complicated system of parts, but a coherent mode of transport).

The role of leaders is to become a crossroads the community always stops at when deciding what it stands for. This they do best by consciously articulating their view of where the organization can go. This is not clarity (ie this is neither the creation nor an imposition of a course) but coherence (ie the firm belief that the organization stands for something to which it must stay true).

Notes

1   If you are looking for a complete biography of Jimmy Wales, the best place to start is Wikipedia itself at http://en.wikipedia.org/wiki/Jimmy_wales.

2   Jimmy Wales Will Destroy Google, an interview by RU Sirius for 10zenmonkeys.com, [Online] 29 January 2007.

3   In many ways Richard Matthew Stallman, who founded the GNU project (the project started to create a Unix-like operating system) and the Free Software Movement (free as in 'free speech' not 'free beer' as defenders of the movement are keen to point out) which became the open source movement, can be credited with starting the collaborative revolution that would make the 'web 2.0' trend possible.

4   Jim Giles (2005) Special Report: Internet encyclopaedias go head to head, *Nature*, **438**, pp 900–01.

5   Jimmy Wales (2005) *Jimmy Wales: How a ragtag band created Wikipedia*, TED talk, Global TED Conference [Online] www.TED.com.

6   For more details on the structure of the Wikipedia community there is no better source than Wikipedia itself. As well as the main encyclopaedia article dealing with Wikipedia, it is worth looking

at the community's functioning by reading some of the entries on the 'About Wikipedia' page or the Community Portal (both can be accessed through links situated on the left-hand side bar of any article).

7   Larry Greenemeier (2007) Wikipedia 'Good Samaritans' are on the money, *Scientific American*, 19 October.

8   The Battle for Wikipedia's Soul, *The Economist Technology Quarterly*, 8 March 2008.

9   Linda Tischler (2005) How to Make Your Products Simpler, *Fast Company*, 14 December.

10   To be fair many commentators would say that lines at Starbucks have increased not as a result of the number of drinks on offer but rather due to the complexity of making some of the non-coffee-based drinks (ie it doesn't matter how many drinks you have, provided they can all be made quickly). This should not, however, deter from the fact that advertising a complex offering is counterintuitive at a time when most seem to agree that we want less rather than more choice.

9 Shift 2 – from plans to narratives

It's not often that you hear an 84-year-old grandmother use the words 'A lot of people like to use dyes, sequins and crap but that's so 1940s. I'm going to show you a kickass technique that's going to be pretty dope'. But Granny Sue is no ordinary 84-year-old. When it comes to explaining how you can customize a pair of sneakers using a wood burning kit or mashing up some tunes at a turntable (ie merging two songs into one), no other words but hers would do. Drinking through a straw from her trademark can of PepsiCo Mountain Dew, Sue was one sweet switched-on granny. She died shortly after recording the first two episodes of her video blog. With condolences flooding her MySpace page she left a big hole in the hearts of the 80,000 or so fans she had amassed on YouTube during her short career. When a video entitled 'Sue Teller R.I.P' mixing a Boys II Men song with clips from her shows was posted online, many a fan heeded the cry of 'Pour some Dew out for Sue' and emptied a can of Mountain Dew in their garden as a sign of affection.

In January 2007, when her recording first appeared on YouTube, Sue Teller was an unknown octogenarian intent on getting young people off their sofas to 'do their own adventures' as her show was called. Despite her humble beginnings and noble cause it was her style that turned her into an internet phenomenon. With camera work and scripts reminiscent of the best of amateur television, Sue's use of street language, her incredible sense of fun and titles such as 'Sue Teller Mashes it Up' and 'Customize Your Kicks', there was every chance that she would be propelled to internet stardom. Sue became a viral phenomenon; the Blentec of grannies. She fulfilled the two conditions we highlighted in Chapter 7 – she was worth talking about and easy to talk about.

The reason I mention Sue is because her work highlights the second critical marker for anyone trying to benefit from the energy of mass collaboration – narrative. If simplicity is about generating the energy that propels a community forward, then narrative is the vector that helps that community move on a coherent path. A narrative helps a community in two ways. First, it clarifies the role of mass collaboration in a business, and second it helps participants align their actions to the delivery of value. Let's take these in turn.

Remember George? His problem was that, on the one hand, Club Penguin offered him a prize (being able to have his own world) but, on the other hand, it didn't offer him the opportunity to decide what he could do with it (being able to write the rules of the game). The same is true with many businesses. The brand (the classic manifestation of a narrative) often promises something that the business cannot deliver. Employees are told that they are the most important asset of the organization but when times are tough some find they are no longer quite so indispensable and are assets that can be disposed off.

Please note, this is not a value judgement on my part. I am not attacking managing a cost base. I am just pointing out the inconsistencies between words and actions. These are what I call narrative inconsistencies. The outcome is either dissatisfaction or cynicism on the part of employees, depending on the nature of the narrative under which they operated. Not only is this dangerous for any business, but more importantly for our purpose, it is counterproductive to any effort to create mass collaboration. The solution is to ensure alignment between the business model and the business narrative. Here is how this plays out with Sue.

The thing is, Granny Sue might not have been quite all she seemed. Following on from the posts on YouTube, a number of media-savvy bloggers sensed that the videos were almost too amateurish. It all felt like the unpolished amateurism was a bit too polished. It had a *Blair Witch Project* feel to it. The fact that the ubiquitous can of Mountain Dew is never very far from sight, mixed with a number of inconsistencies (such as her MySpace page declaring that she was 89 and the R.I.P video released showing her as 84 at the time of her death), made people wonder if this could be another 'fideo' (ie a fake video – a fairly usual occurrence in the world of YouTube viral marketing). As a result of their investigations many bloggers went on to speculate that Granny Sue's videos were not those of an amateur video blogger but rather might well be a piece of viral marketing produced by Pepsi Co to be used in the run up to their Super Bowl advertising campaign. The plot thickened when avid viewers of Current TV (the 24/7 channel mentioned in Chapter 4) spotted that during the credit sequence of the Mash-Up video the words 'promotional consideration has been paid for by Mountain Dew' appeared. Could Granny Sue be the new LonelyGirl15?

Another YouTube and MySpace phenomenon, LonelyGirl15 made her first appearance in her video blog on 16 June 2006. Bree, a 16-year-old teenager, decided that it would be fun to record slices of her life to post on YouTube. She created her username, LonelyGirl15, invested in a webcam and soon began talking meaningfully to herself about meaningless events, posted for all to watch. So far nothing unusual about that; there are plenty of lonely girls and boys on YouTube! But Bree's posts became very popular. And that's when questions started.

Given so many video bloggers out there, how did this one in particular become so popular? Sure her username might have attracted a few hopeful boys to start with, but the video had to be good enough for them to want to come back. And Bree was indeed very funny, sweet, provocative and intelligent and whatever else she needed to be to attract an ever-growing audience. As we saw in Chapter 7, by being worth talking about, Bree had made herself a prime candidate for viral status. This is all interesting but not of interest for us here, until you find that, like Sue Teller, questions started to be raised about how genuine she really was.

Suspicious viewers smelled a hoax. What made the posts so compelling also made the musings of a 16-year-old seem a little less than genuine. It all felt like very smart, clever writing. It was Matt Foremski, the 18-year-old son of a reporter for the blog 'Silicon Valley Watcher', who first raised the alarm when he discovered photos of Bree going under a different name. Detective work ensued and eventually 16-year-old LonelyGirl15, the home-schooled daughter of strictly religious parents, was outed as 20-year-old Jessica Rose, a New Zealand-born US actress. This was not necessarily a bad thing (at least an actress brings an element of quality to her interaction with a camera) nor illegal (taking on a different identity is often encouraged when posting on public forums). But what made Bree a cause célèbre wasn't the form of her posts but rather the intent.

As *The New York Times* was eventually to claim, the issue was that 'Lonely Girl (and Friends) Just Wanted a Movie Deal'.[1] That was the really deceitful bit. It's OK (even if mildly embarrassing) to be interested in a 16-year-old girl talking about her life. It's pretty common to enjoy watching a series in which an actress pretends to be someone else (that's her job). What felt wrong to the 70 million or so combined viewers was the deceit of pretending to be something you are not. You end up feeling pretty cheated or stupid when you realize that a 16-year-old's diatribes are in fact written by three men (who happened to be a screenwriter turned director, a surgical residency drop-out turned filmmaker and a former attorney turned, well, former attorney). That hurts.

The narrative is broken. By narrative I mean the construct that helps explain a sequence of events and your place within it. In this case the narrative of LonelyGirl15 was 'I am an amateur blogger who will talk about the events that will shape my life and I invite you to listen and comment. I open my normal world to you.' It is not a complex narrative. The LonelyGirl narrative is no Greek tragedy but it is an honest and simple narrative. It is certainly a different narrative from 'I am an aspiring actress working under a non-disclosure agreement with three middle-aged aspiring filmmakers who hope to get a movie-making deal'. There is nothing wrong with that narrative if that's what I had bought, but in this case it was the former that was for sale.

The word 'narrative' comes from the Latin verb *narrare*, meaning to 'recount', and is related to the adjective *gnarus*, meaning 'knowing' (derived from the root *to know*). In that sense the narrative tells us what we need to know and clarifies our relationship with these video blogs. The reason you feel cheated when you discover that LonelyGirl is in fact an actress, or that Granny Sue is the human face of a global soft drinks company (although the jury is still out on that one), is because you have adjusted the nature of your relationship with their stories to fit the narrative. You have posted comments you felt were responses to a genuine girl's concerns. You have poured out your Mountain Dew because you felt you were paying your respects to a granny, not to a corporation. As the narrative unfolded so did your relationship with it, including your actions. When this narrative profoundly changes, the role you had previously adopted (ie your character) no longer fits in. You were the voyeur of a normal life and suddenly you are asked to become one of the audience for a scripted story.

For some, the dishonesty of finding out that the narrative they followed was in fact a fraud is enough to make them reject the story. They switched off, never to log on again. Others simply accepted this new narrative and adjusted their behaviour accordingly (no longer commenting on the sadness of Bree's life but focusing instead on the production value of the video for example). One blogger commenting about whether or not Granny Sue was real said 'who cares'. Clearly he didn't. The narrative for Sue wasn't about whether or not she was a corporate instrument. The narrative was that a cool granny was worth watching. Whether or not Sue was a PepsiCo Granny did not matter that much – she was still an elderly woman switched on to youth culture and for some people, that was enough. Once you accept a new narrative you are willing to put energy into the new story.

This explains why LonelyGirl15 has not disappeared despite having been outed. It seems that our protagonists got their wish after all. LonelyGirl15 became a very successful online series. Like all series it has its own spinoff (KateModern, featuring the art of Kate first screened on Bebo – another social networking site – in July 2007). Jessica Rose has become a United Nations goodwill ambassador. She has appeared on an ABC show. The series *Law and Order* screened a story inspired by the events. Artists and magazines have used the story and Carmen Electra even spoofed the show. This is undoubtedly a pretty good outcome for a show built on deceit and product placement (the show was the first to use product placement in online social media, featuring Hershey's Icebreaker Sours Gum and Neutrogena). At the time of writing these words, the creators of LonelyGirl15 had secured US$5 million in VC funding for their next projects.

So, back to our organizations. Currently, an organization's brand is the main incarnation of its narrative. It helps consumers decide the nature of their relationship with the organization. Apple is not immune to issues with its products (every release is usually accompanied by hundreds of forum entries related to user problems) yet it seems to escape the criticism Microsoft receives. This is not an argument about whose products are better or more stable (I know better than to enter into any argument about Apple with its fan base) but simply a recognition of the power of narratives.

If your brand positioning is that your products are all about innovation and design in support of a simplified user experience, many people will forgive the teething problems (everybody knows innovation is not always perfect) as long as the design is genuinely groundbreaking. If, on the other hand, engineering on a grand scale is your bag, you're unlikely ever to get anywhere if your product doesn't work 100 per cent of the time. 'Where do you want to go today?', the question Microsoft asked of all of us, takes on a whole different meaning when your web browser doesn't want to load and certainly warrants a different response than the 'think different' Apple promised.

There is no right or wrong narrative, as we adapt our actions and reactions to that which is relevant to us. What doesn't work is when we are asked to react to a narrative that calls for another reaction. Let's go back to the car example of the previous chapter. If your car doesn't want to start in the morning, your reaction will be different depending on whether you are setting off for work or for a vacation (in my experience, either one can be a relief depending on the length of the journey and the number of children in the car).

This first rule of narratives (that they help us define our involvement in a social process) is only one side of the coin. Narratives do much more than that. As we saw in Chapter 6, in mass collaboration no one seems to be in control. And if no one is in control, how can the organization ensure that any mass collaboration effort actually delivers value? The fear a leader experiences when faced with the logic of 'crowdsourcing' is legitimate. The answer to that problem still lies with Sue. The narrative is the source of social alignment. It is the story participants build that helps them fulfil the engagement created by simplicity. A narrative environment helps people orientate their effort. Here is how it works.

During the past decade, researchers have looked at how insects, despite their lack of intelligence and awareness, still manage to behave in a way that appears social. Whilst at a cursory glance each insect seems to have its own agenda, the colony as a whole still looks coordinated. They all seem to be moving together (they seem aligned) despite the absence of leadership or supervisory control. The mechanism they use to coordinate their actions is relatively simple to describe – by leaving traces in its environment, one insect stimulates the performance of an action by another insect. This process is called stigmergy.

The term was first introduced by French biologist Pierre-Paul Grassé in 1959 to refer to the apparently social behaviour of termites. Deriving the word from the Greek words *stigma* (sign) and *ergon* (action), Grassé sought to explain the idea of agents' actions leaving signs in the environment. Whilst this might seem like hard work, Grassé was not averse to big projects, having started in 1946 the *Traité de Zoologie*, the 38 volumes of which would require him almost 40 years to complete.

In 1982 he composed his labour of love for termites. The *Termitologia*, with its three volumes and over 2,400 pages, is a must-read if you ever want to know everything there is to know about termites. It also contains the findings that are important to us. In it, Grassé explains how termites deposit pheromones in the mud balls they use to construct their nests. These pheromone deposits attract other termites who, as a result, deposit their mud balls in close proximity. The process repeats itself (ie every time an agent comes into contact with these signs they too adapt their actions) until their amazingly intricate mounds are built. Far be it for me to compare human beings to termites, but, truth is, we're not averse to a bit of stigmergy ourselves!

A year or so ago I was told a story by a colleague of mine that has stayed with me ever since. Like many stories we tell each other over the water cooler this one was sworn to be true, happened to a close friend (in this case her brother) and cannot be substantiated by any research I tried to conduct since. However, I neither doubt her good faith nor does it actually matter if the details are accurate.[2] It goes something like this.

Two Canadian universities (names withheld to protect the innocent) undertook major building programmes at the same time. When it came to laying down the paths one of the universities' presidents sat down with the architects and contractors to painstakingly design the best paths. The other president took a different approach. He just asked the contractors to postpone laying paths for a year. The delay wasn't welcomed by the workers, who were operating on a tight schedule, but they reluctantly agreed.

One year later, the president asked the lead architect to come up with him on a helicopter ride with the overall site plans. As they gained altitude he just pointed down at the natural paths students had carved into the lawns by repeatedly walking across the same grass. Looking at the puzzled architects he then said, 'These muddy areas are where we'll have our paths'.

What visitors to these two universities can now witness is one Canadian university with beautiful, logically laid but never-used paths and a lot of muddy lines, and another university with well-trodden paved paths and beautiful lawns.

What this story points to is the difference between a plan and a narrative environment. The logic of the plan set out by the architect and president of the first university was irrevocable. The paths took the shortest and most logical route between each building. In an organization analogy, the paths were designed at the ultimate point of efficiency. In leadership terms the architect and the presidents were beyond reproach. We may look at them now and point to a failure in planning but with the benefit of hindsight, everyone can be a good planner.

The president of the second university understood that plans imposed on a community only *appear* efficient. They make a leader feel in control and reward us with a sense of decisive action. The truth is somewhat more complicated. As long as we have no way of second guessing the future, a plan can never be efficient. After all, we know that the real experts in laying paths are the people who walk on them. A communal narrative environment is much more likely to help us involve them than a plan. The good news for leaders is that we willingly follow the paths others have trodden.

Termite-mound engineering seems like a silly idea – better let them do their own thing rather than endeavour to move termites one at a time in order to build a mound that looks like the Taj Mahal. Remember, our termites are engaged, we ensured they were through our efforts at simplicity, so we don't have to worry about their willingness to contribute, we only need them to align their efforts. And for that, we might as well let stigmergy take its course given that it is a highly effective and efficient way to build mounds.

A narrative environment is a place where stories unfold. It can be a physical environment (as with the example of the university grounds) or a conceptual environment (as with Bree's life or Granny Sue's adventures). The narrative environment gives us the space we need to explore and enact the story. I like to use the word narrative rather than story as we have come to intimately link stories with fiction and the term has been overused if not abused in recent business contexts. Important cultural artefacts, however, help us orientate our behaviour through the lessons they teach. Narrative environments are the places within which this coordination takes place.

Cultural-historical psychologists study how individual human intelligence develops in interaction with people and the environment. They postulate that human beings inhabit an environment transformed by the activity of prior members of their species. These transformations pass from one generation to the next through physical or cultural artefacts that help us coordinate our activities in social ways. Sounds like termites and pheromones to me!

Narratives help us focus and align. That's why children the world over (and a few adults too) accomplish complex actions through talking to themselves while they work. By doing so, they develop narratives that help them modify their understanding of the problem at hand and facilitate their search for a solution. They deposit conceptual pheromones along the natural pathways of their minds to create logical, well-laid and efficient paths. They do not have a plan to go from problem to solution. Instead they create a narrative that helps them make sense of the world around them in search of the best solution. It is that capacity for sense-making that makes communities so incredibly efficient. Free from interference, the processes they use for inquiry create the most efficient and sustainable way to get from A to B.

Let's move away from the viral world of marketing and the academic world of biology and see how these things play out in the world of organizations. The open systems we looked at in the early chapters of this book showed complex, adaptive and reactive structures without the control, planning and even communications afforded by traditional organizations. Each member of the system is both attracted to contribute by adopting a role in the community (master, shaper, participant, dependent or rebel) and able to adapt that role to align behind the delivery of the value demanded by the community. We saw in the last chapter how this attraction to the communal aims is not the result of strategically induced clarity but rather the result of simplicity.

What the characters we have introduced in this chapter (from Sue to termites) show us is that the adaptation of agents towards the delivery of value is more efficiently achieved via the facilitation of a narrative environment than the construction of a plan. Remember, whether faced with a plan or not (ie whether or not there are well-paved, logical paths for us to use), we use the clues we gain from the artefacts in the narrative environment (physical and conceptual) to adapt our behaviour (ie we go for the muddy ones every time).

This process of adoption and adaptation that leads to alignment is the process we try to replicate as leaders in traditional organizations through imposing structure and control. Don't get me wrong, our fears are well founded. There are plenty of instances of organizations failing because employees or customers refuse to align. These failures, however, are not the results of sabotage on the part of awkward human resources, or a failure in planning. They are simply the symptoms of narrative inconsistencies. The wrong causal diagnostic invariably leads to the wrong remedy being put in place.

What is our alignment modus operandi in organizations? When we talk about aligning resources behind the delivery of value or objectives, we look to provide a route for the organization to take that will be as efficient as possible. In this case, efficiency means being able to accomplish a task to the highest standard for the minimum cost in the minimum time. It is to achieve this efficiency that we build plans.

Plans are formulated in a way that describes a logical series of steps that will take us from A (where we are now) to B (our strategic intent). These ensure anyone knows what their role is and how that role fits within a bigger picture. This is a long-winded way to describe a process with which we are all familiar. It goes something like this. Our strategic objective is to grow by 10 per cent. The way we are going to get there is through innovative products. Your role as a sales person is to get us the best possible deals so we can invest in product development. That's a pretty clear plan and your role as a leader is to monitor the fulfilment of the plan, all the while minimizing costly deviations and maximizing operational improvements. This kind of termite-mound engineering is as good as it gets.

The problem is that most of our time as leaders is invariably spent on trying to manage the consequences of pheromone attraction. We believe people are awkward and non-compliant. We cajole ourselves, knowing that this annoyance is what we're paid to manage and we try to get on with the job, when in fact people are being efficient in sensing and responding to their ever-changing environment.

Think about the difference between plans and narrative environments this way. I am sure this scenario has happened to you. You're walking down a busy street and suddenly you do that little shuffle people do when someone is coming the other way and neither of you can decide whether to go left or right. That's what I call the planning shuffle.

Next time it happens to you, notice how it started when, for a brief moment, you interrupted your journey to stare at the other person, suddenly realizing their presence on a collision course with your path. It was at that stage that you thought through what steps you would take (literally) to avoid them. That cursive glance you exchanged also meant that they too formulated a course of action. And your combined lack of imagination or the availability of only two strategic options encouraged a few missteps. That's what happens when you formulate a plan.

You could formulate an entire plan to take you from the beginning of your street to the shop you need to go to. Indeed, when we search for something specific in places we don't know, we do just that. In fact, it is when we walk with our heads up, trying to follow our plan, that we are most likely to catch someone else's eyes and shuffle. Plans generate shuffles and shuffles are not efficient! A plan as used in organizations to secure alignment is just like that. You describe every single step.

In most cases, however, when we go shopping we restrict our plans to what others have called 'the commander's intent'. The expression 'the commander's intent' identifies the military's way of thinking that any strategy ceases to be useful the moment you reach the battlefield, as most of what will happen is unpredictable. Therefore it is better to describe the goal of the mission and let soldiers get on with the rest.

Back to your shopping trip. It is not a plan (I will take three steps left and four right) nor is it a goal (I need to be at the store) that gets you efficiently from A to B. It is a rich narrative that does it. It is that need to get that present for your daughter's birthday that you know will raise a smile bright enough to light the route a shuttle could take from here to the Moon. It is you imagining the weeks of anticipation she has gone through and the day of the birthday party where all the anticipation will finally be realized. That narrative ensures that you navigate your way along 'Main Street' avoiding shuffles as you adjust your behaviour against the commander's intent (assuming your daughter, like mine, can easily fulfil the role of commander in your family). The narrative environments we inhabit facilitate our achievement of goals, not the plans we formulate.

The role of the leader is not to design plans, rather it is to help the organization construct a narrative by nurturing the narrative environment. It sounds a bit more woolly but it's a whole lot more effective. Nurturing a narrative environment (ie being a president who can let muddy paths point to the right way) is about helping the organization acquire a tone.

The tone of the organization is the type of story it will tell. Is the story of your department, your function, your organization one of conflict or is it a story of change and cooperation? Is it a story of survival or one of growth? To nurture a tone forces a leader to understand the key moments in organizational life and frame these in a way that clarifies their significance. What are the key moments in your communal life? What is the beat of your business? Of course meetings and deadlines provide the rhythm to any organization, but think about this more broadly in terms of narrative. What are the moments that need to be highlighted in the life of your community?

Nurturing a tone is about creating a sense of place for the community. It is about linking the small tasks that make up the life of an organization into the overall rhythm of the community. To do so means finding the key words that will give tone to the story. Here we need to be careful. This is not about the leader spinning some news into something big or trying to write a story. Remember, the role of the leader is limited to nurturing the narrative environment. So rather than writing the words, this is about helping use the key words the community is transmitting.

A good example of the ability to focus on the key words and the mood that help the narrative environment is Twitter. Twitter was created by Obvious (a San Francisco-based company) in 2006 and has become one of the fastest-growing social networking applications. Twitter is a service that helps people stay connected by exchanging short, frequent answers to one simple question: What are you doing? In Twitter people use 140 characters or less to update others on what they are up to. They update their status throughout the day whether they are 'getting to work' or 'struggling with getting the kids ready' or even 'trying to solve some big IT problem'. Whatever it is, their Twitter status helps forge connections between a disparate community.

Now transpose this idea to the workplace and you have Yammer. Instead of resting on some publicly accessible server, Yammer aims to provide the same functionality that has proved so popular on Twitter, but this time on the enterprise server. Basically, it takes anyone sharing a similar e-mail address and links them together. There are two reasons why, despite having won the TechCrunch 50 awards, it is a fair bet to assume that Yammer will never be Twitter.

The first is that Yammer doesn't have the 140-word limit. You would have thought this would be a plus but it isn't. The 140-word limit is Twitter's killer app. Everyone in organizations has e-mail. They could use it to update anyone else. But the 140 words force you to decide what is important. When you are faced with the attention trend, the 140 words is what helps separate the narrative from the noise. The fact is that someone in a conversation has to separate signal from noise.

The second problem is in the democratic trend. Most of us want to be able to update our status in the knowledge that not everyone in the organizational ecosystem sees it. Sure Yammer is a good application but it is not a narrative-building application.

Remember Jimbo in the last chapter. His key ability is to put the words of the community in perspective. This is the ability to link the different words the participants use into a tone for the overall organization. It is essential for creating a flow that can guide individuals through the narrative of the organization.

So what does all this look like in practice? First the leader must help the community identify its tone. This is done by focusing on three key questions. Who are we (ie who you and I are and where we come from and what we stand for)? Where are we going (ie why you and I are here and what we aim to get from our relationship)? Why are we going there (ie what is it that you and I can do together that cannot be done more effectively by anyone else)?

Once these questions become a mantra in the organization, the role of the leader is to connect the key moments in the organization with the key words in the overall narrative. Think about your part of the organization like a comic strip. What are the key frames? Which of the events do you use to provide the organization with focus? Remember that the source of your power is the community. The community's members give you legitimacy, so using that power to give focus to their words and actions in order to make the community more effective at achieving its aims is what this focus creation is about. Having established the frames that matter you now have a narrative environment. What your position affords you is the ability to communicate the words that matter in shaping that environment to a broader community. The leader is the mouthpiece of the organization not its creator.

We now have engagement through simplicity and the chance to achieve alignment through narratives but how do we ensure that the effort is focused? How do we ensure that everyone has accountabilities that will make the organization effort successful? Accountabilities are the lifeblood of operational excellence so how do they work in open organizations? Let me take you on a small trip through space to find out.

The 30 second recap

The second building block to any organizational effort, after engagement, is alignment. Leaders must answer two critical questions.

How do I ensure that community members understand their involvement in the social process (ie how do they best contribute)? And how do I make sure that people stay aligned behind the mission?

Both of these are normally answered with a plan. But as plans will invariably become obsolete in the face of change, it is better to have a community able to make sense of the evolving environment and respond appropriately to changes. This is achieved through narrative environments that enable free exploration of options whilst retaining an intact notion of the overall mission.

The role of the leader is to facilitate the narrative – helping participants and the community define who they are, what they aspire to and how they hope to get there.

Notes

1   Virginia Heffernan and Tom Zeller (2006) The Lonely Girl That Really Wasn't, *New York Times*, 13 September.
2   I actually came across the story again recently, this time in *Brain Rules*, the fantastic book by John Medina exposing how our brain works. Medina recounts hearing the story told by a speaker at a university conference and describes it as an urban legend. Either he is right or my friend's brother was that university speaker. Who knows?

10 Shift 3 – from roles to tasks

It seems nothing can stop our relentless fascination with and search for extra-terrestrial life. Far from being the stuff of science fiction, the area that quickly became known as SETI (Search for Extra-Terrestrial Intelligence) has entered the realm of mainstream, government-sponsored science. The methodology underpinning much of the search is simple. Instead of staring mindlessly into the sky, researchers listen for any potential radio transmission (and I don't mean some kind of alien FM) coming from outer space. This is a book about mass collaboration and it doesn't come more exciting than this, for here too you can participate.

Here is how. In May 1999, UC Berkeley launched a new project – SETI@home – funded by The Planetary Society, The State of California and, unsurprisingly given the potential discovery, Paramount Pictures. The way it works is simple. To become part of the research all you have to do is download the SETI@home software and you are on. In layman's terms (the only ones I am familiar with I am afraid), what the software does is use the processing power of your computer whenever you are not using it. The more people get involved, the more computing power becomes available to analyse the signals from outer space in search of potential intelligence.

The project quickly became popular. By 2008, there were over 5 million computers linked together to form a network located in 226 countries and contributing the equivalent of over 2 million years of processing time.[1] And if that all sounds a bit too wacky for you, wait until I tell you that these millions of linked-up computers have actually found something interesting. They heard a signal they named SHGb02+14a (in that inimitable way scientists have of giving catchy and easily remembered names to things). Even if Dan Werthimer, Chief Scientist for SETI@home, says 'We're not jumping up and down, but we are continuing to observe it,' and David Anderson, Director of SETI@home, concludes that 'It's unlikely to be real but we will definitely be re-observing it,'[2] this is still an interesting development. You may argue that one unusual signal seems like very little for such a big endeavour but even without signals SETI@home still matters to us.

The reason it matters is this. SETI@home is an example of how the expertise trend is changing one of our key leadership levers in a profound way. Not only are intellectual and social capitals now distributed (ie outside the boundaries of a corporation) but SETI@home has no control over its prime resource – computing capacity. The benefits this brings were unimaginable only a few years ago. In fact, at a time when major US and Japanese corporations were investing millions of dollars in trying to build the world's largest supercomputer, SETI@home was beating them hands down by being able to perform operations at about twice the speed of their fastest efforts. This concept of capital distribution isn't just applied to aliens. It is being extended to other areas of research like cancer.

For leaders the consequences of such models are profound. We looked at the need for engagement and alignment as being critical to any organization. We also know that accountabilities make or break co-creation efforts. In this distributed model, where do accountabilities lie? How do you ensure the accountability is fulfilled?

As the participant whose computer detected SHGb02+14a put it when wondering how his employer might react to his work computer having been used for extra-terrestrial search purposes: 'I might have to explain a little further about just how much I was using the computers'.[3] You may argue that by being distributed, accountabilities are shared. After all, his is only one of many computers that form the network and, as his actions were limited to the download of what is effectively only a screensaver, so his personal accountability to the project is minimized. Now imagine, however, if, as well as using your computer, SETI@home also used you. That would sharpen the accountability somewhat. Well, we don't even have to imagine. This is happening now.

Just down the hall from the SETI@home headquarters, Andrew Westphal, a planetary scientist, was working on space dust. He was trying to find particles of a certain kind which, even though a trained eye could find them, computers could not detect. His problem was rather big, literally. Westphal would have to look at millions of pictures if he ever wanted to make progress. How do you get more eyes?[4]

He wasn't the only one asking that question. Producing detailed maps of Mars is an arduous task but finding out about crater markings is key to, amongst other things, producing age maps to get a better understanding of the planet. But there too, the Westphal problem occurred. The question facing NASA Mars scientists was how do you produce detailed maps of craters when you have literally millions of pictures and only two eyes?

What NASA and Westphal figured out was that they could use the same trick as SETI@home did. They could enlist you and me. They realized that whilst some scientific tasks require deep expertise, others are mainly about looking at things with a bit of training and a lot of common sense. Identifying craters on Mars and detecting space particles fall into that latter category. Enter 'the clickworkers'.[5]

From November 2000 to September 2001, NASA ran an experiment to see if volunteers (clickworkers) working on their home computers for as little as a few minutes a day could conduct the task of crater mapping, which was normally the preserve of graduate students. The

Clickworkers programme presented a series of images from which participants were asked to identify and measure the diameter of Mars's craters. SETI@home and the Clickworkers projects became the inspiration for Westphal's Stardust@home, through which volunteers provide brain rather than computer power to identify particles. The results were startling.

These efforts at what has come to be known as 'citizen science' provided results beyond anyone's expectations. In its first six months of operation, more than 85,000 people became clickworkers. Together they made more than 1.9 million entries. But were they any good? Are clickworkers as good as experts? Having looked at the power of the expertise trend before, we can guess the answer. Data from NASA shows that the efforts of volunteers are largely comparable to those of trained experts. Of course, there are scientific experiments that require a vast amount of knowledge and training that no volunteer will be able to undertake. However, NASA has effectively outsourced what was expert work to our living rooms, thereby releasing the precious time of experts to concentrate on other things. And it is working![6]

Now let's think about the accountability issue again. This time it is not just your computer that matters, but your devotion to the work. In organizations we use roles to define a set of accountabilities. At its simplest, a role is a collection of inputs (eg skills and knowledge), throughputs (ie the act of transforming something using the input) and outputs (ie the results). We could safely use a similar approach for clickworkers. We know what the three variables are so we can develop a set of expectations about clickworkers and build accountabilities necessary for the organization's smooth running within these roles. In this sense the role becomes a set of expectations.

But the concept of a role as a repository of accountability is not enough. We also need to ensure roles drive the desire to be accountable. After all, there is nothing in the clickworker role that makes it likely to be performed other than the desire of an individual to fulfil the accountabilities. So whilst it may be possible to develop a role description for a clickworker, the valuable quest is to give them a role they perceive to be fulfilling enough to want to do it.

We need to find out what is driving their sense of accountability. We need to find a way to recreate the hackneyed and more than likely made-up story of the stonemason proudly declaring he wasn't just carving a stone but building a cathedral. In fact, let's stay with that one for a little while and go back in time to fifteenth-century medieval Europe.

Legend has it that a child named Jacques learnt to carve stones early on in his childhood and eventually left his home, aged fifteen, to work in the trade. We find him again, aged 36, this time known as Master Jacques, on the site of the building of the Temple of Solomon, where he was heading up the stonecutters, carpenters and masons divisions. The legend of Master Jacques, rich in the kind of intrigue that would make *The Da Vinci Code* pale with envy, is a great story to tell but matters little to us here. The important thing is that the legend of Master Jacques led to the development of a community (the *compagnonnage*) that can teach us a lot about accountabilities.

The 'compagnonnage' movement was the start of the European guild system where craftsmen would congregate to form associations in order to exchange knowledge and skills. To become a master craftsman, and therefore able to belong to the guild, required an apprenticeship that would go through numerous stages. To fulfil these stages, the aspiring master would become a journeyman, travelling the length and breadth of Europe in search of knowledge and projects on which to develop his skills. Eventually, this training would culminate in the production of a masterpiece (the best possible example of his work), which would be judged by masters to determine whether the apprentice was fit to become a master himself.

It is no coincidence that I use the term 'masters' to describe the people who make today's communities function, for the parallels are easy to see. The fact that open communities rely on reputation, capability and craftsmanship is a testament to a model developed all those centuries ago. Much like the communities I studied for this book, these European guilds evoke the coming together of people for the purpose of sharing knowledge, educating others, cooperating and collaborating. It is also worthy of note that the term 'compagnon' (which identified the stages of the apprenticeship of a journeyman) finds its roots in the popular Latin 'companio', the term that describes 'breaking bread with a friend'. Journeymen would be hosted on their travels by fellow tradesmen who would teach them their skills. The journey was not only one of development but of a rite of passage towards acceptance. But what has that got to do with roles and your leadership?

What the 'compagnonnage' example gives us is an understanding of roles as more than a construct needed for the fulfilment of accountabilities. The role of journeyman defined a person's life. It had symbolic aspects that individuals used to define who they were and how they chose to live their lives. The role was more than a set of organizational requirements – it was a powerful source of personal identity.

Roles in effect contain two different types of constructs. One is a set of expectations and accountabilities placed on an individual by the community for the purpose of fulfilling an outcome. That is very much the construct we have in mind when using roles to define accountabilities in an organization. By defining a role, we define a set of behaviours we expect the role holder to display. The other is the role we see ourselves fulfilling in a social context. That role, far from being defined and given, evolves through an interactive process (starting in childhood) of responding and adapting to our environment. That role helps us develop our self-image.

Think about it in SETI@home terms. What is your role when you are co-opted into the search? Are you an engineer? Are you a pioneer? Are you a computer geek or a dreaming adventurer? The choice, quite frankly, is yours – the accountability of downloading a piece of software is only a mechanism towards becoming what you set out to be.

There are therefore two aspects we need to focus on to understand how followers embrace accountabilities. One is defined by a series of tasks the community needs to have fulfilled in order to be sustainable. The other is a series of expectations individuals have about the nature of their contribution. To embrace their accountabilities fully, individuals look for alignment between organizational expectations (tasks, norms and required behaviours) and their self-image (ie the place they want in the company). And this is where we hit a problem.

In his book *The Corrosion of Character*, sociologist Richard Sennett tells the story of a Boston bakery. The job of the baker is hard. The hot ovens burn the bakers whilst the dough-beater pulls their muscles. The long night shifts destroy their family lives whilst the long hours destroy their health. You would have thought this environment would more than welcome automation.

When a conglomerate purchased the old Greek Bakery, machines were quickly introduced. At the touch of a button, a baker could programme any kind of bread production. Italian breads, French breads and all other kinds of exotic breads could be produced. Whatever shape or colour anyone wanted only required punching the right set of buttons on the central computer. No more hot, heavy, smelly, tiresome work for the bakers of Boston. The opportunity to produce numerous varieties to meet changing tastes also met with customers' approval. What more could anyone want?

The answer to that is simple – the bakers wanted to, once again, bake bread! Sennett remarks how the bakers experienced confusion in their status. They longed to be bakers once again, rather than machine operators. He tells the story of one baker saying that when he gets home at night, he actually bakes bread to regain the pride he once had in the work he did.

The identity of the bakers is now diluted by the machines. Where once they had pride and felt accountable for their work, they have now been removed from the work itself and only feel alienation and indifference. Whilst automation might have made their work bearable it had made their lives unbearable. Whilst the organization had clarified and ensured accountabilities, the disappearance of the company (literally in their case as they no longer shared bread) had made them unable to see themselves as accountable. The duties they were now being asked to fulfil as part of their roles no longer aligned with their self-image. This dissonance between role and self-image always leads to conflict. Their role as bakery operators rather than bakers made them unable to commit fully to either. As a result they no longer knew which behaviours to adopt or accountabilities to fulfil.

This is not merely a story of automation in the baking industry – it is the precursor to a world in the midst of our trends. The demographic trend means that self-image is becoming ever more important as an entire generation no longer identifies with organizations. The expertise trend is making it ever harder for one organization to define a coherent role when the accountabilities are multiple and distributed throughout a network. The attention trend is making organizations less and less relevant to the building of social roles and norms as the tools for identity-building available to all increase exponentially. The democratic trend is making it harder for leaders to take a primary role in the definition of role and self-image.

As generations learn to define themselves by an ever broader range of activities outside organizations and work contexts, creating account-ability for a co-creation effort will require a new set of tools. To use the language we introduced in the last chapter, the simplification of the bakers' work has left a void of coherence that has decreased their ability to embrace their accountabilities.

This conflict between the role we are required to play and the role we are looking to fulfil is the source of many of the social dysfunctions we are starting to experience in the workplace. When we are in a cohesive company with mutual reinforcement of group norms, we not only make the group but also ourselves stronger. But when our group and personal identities become separated we find ourselves in a state of constant flux and dissatisfaction. The apparent conflict between work and life and the rejection by a new generation of what has been seen as meaningless hierarchies bears witness to that conflict. So how do we establish a sense of accountability in such an environment? The truth is not only that we can't but, more importantly, that we shouldn't.

When we look to create a sense of accountability in others we invariably try to influence their behaviour by manipulating the environment in which they work. As we recognize that, in and of itself, an organizational role only defines the accountability, we look to apply social norms as a way to make people want to fulfil them. This is when we use the 'our organization will save the world' philosophy exposed previously.

We assume that people will put up with anything if they derive meaning from a bigger aim. We try to make our stonecutters believe that they are building cathedrals. In practice it means that we try to manipulate both the cultural environment (through incentives, rewards and punishments) as well as the individuals themselves (through performance appraisals and development discussions) towards a state where we hope they will recognize the importance of the accountabilities to the fulfilment of their lives' purpose. This represents much wasted effort as it is unlikely that our actions alone will generate sufficient buy-in to eradicate the role conflicts embedded in our trends.

The more fruitful strategy for leaders is to recognize that, in fact, it is the tasks themselves rather than the role that need fulfilment. In a Linux or a Wikipedia there are many tasks that need completing which do not necessarily belong in anyone's role. These are completed because individuals who define themselves through the community's existence would do anything to make it strong, irrespective of whether or not they are accountable for these tasks through their role. If the task doesn't get fulfilled, the community no longer functions.

Think about a project you have been involved in or you have witnessed. When a project team is brought together, usually to work on something outside the normal everyday function of the organization, people pull together in a way seldom seen. It is as though the project team has an energy all of its own that carries it forward. People cooperate and collaborate, picking up tasks along the way irrespective of whether these form part of their role description. This is not due to some novelty somehow built into projects, or some group normative technique that distorts the reality of the menial nature of a particular task. It is simply because the usual process has been reversed. Instead of having to fulfil a role that fits into a bigger picture, bounded project teams have as their primary purpose the fulfilment of the bigger picture. Let me put it another way.

The focus of a leader has traditionally been on organizational account-abilities that emphasize role requirements. In practice this means that we build roles that together represent the accountabilities suffi-cient for the delivery of the purpose. We then endeavour to have employees fulfil these accountabilities to the best of their abilities with a combination of reinforcement and corrective activities. This reliance on role requirements accompanied by social engineering has served us well. It has enabled us to get a culture of accountability to flow through the organizational system and, with skilful leaders, has even resulted in the release of discretionary effort on the part of some employees.

However, this book is about the world of mass participation created by the DEAD trends. These trends no longer allow for roles to be the primary drivers of accountability. Leaders in the post-DEAD trends world need to focus on community (ie company rather than organization) accountabilities, emphasizing task completion. In practice this means working with the community to determine the tasks necessary for success and helping individuals in the completion of these tasks in line with their image.

Of course you can argue that a collection of tasks is overly haphazard. You could suggest that it is too piecemeal to fit the requirements of complex creation efforts. Even if we discount the fact that even in the best organizations the average employee only spends about 11 minutes on an activity before being disrupted,[7] this is a valid concern. But we need to remember that the concept of accountability is only critical as a driver currently because we have little else to ensure that our requirements are delivered when the social role and the organizational role are conflicted.

In a world where the social role drives the creation effort (ie a world where people want to be accountable for the success of the company) the need to drive accountabilities becomes less of a concern. That is not to say that roles will disappear – this is unlikely. But their prevalence in the creation effort will be less. Even in complex industrial environments, we will need to realize that the roles we develop are only necessary for us to organize the process of creativity, they will not be (and arguably seldom have been) the driver of a culture of accountability.

It is not for leaders, therefore, to struggle to reconcile the role conflict between the organizational role and the individual's self-image. What the leader is there to do is to facilitate the creation of coherence by letting community members create that logic for themselves whilst reinforcing the need of the community. The best way to do this is to focus on clear task definition.

At this stage in the argument we should have already secured both the engagement and the alignment of any member of the community. We have the simplicity and the narrative we need to transform the organization in a company. Tasks are the critical incidents that move the narrative along. Of course, there is no denying that the organization needs roles; after all, roles are its foundations. However, the reinforcement of the social roles of individuals born out of their self-image can only be accomplished through tasks. It is therefore a change of emphasis in a leader's dialogue that needs to take place.

When tasks are well defined, time bound and necessary, they form the words in the company's narrative. Who wouldn't want to stare at dust particles if they always wanted to be a space explorer? Who wouldn't want to carve a stone when they are dedicated to building a cathedral, and what point is there in wasting energy by constantly reminding the cutter that they are building a cathedral, when what they really need is help in producing the best possible carving to make their contribution the best it can be?

The fact is that in order to fulfill their self-image, people will choose to complete tasks that make the community sustainable. Some of these will be what we may want to call accountability tasks (ie going to the immediate fulfilment of the organizational purpose) whilst others might be best described as maintenance tasks (ie tasks that are contributory to the fulfilment of accountability tasks).

Clearly, when looking at organizations without a shift in mindset this kind of strategy seems rather complicated or haphazard. Does it mean we should somehow have an auction of who does what task or, even worse, let people choose and run the risk of having tasks left incomplete? In reality the practice is not that different from what currently happens except that it is now acknowledged and discussed. First there is nothing currently, even in the most coercive environments, to stop an individual making a choice of, at the very least, how much of their energy they will invest in a task (which in turn will have a direct impact on the quality of that task's completion).

But second, and perhaps more fundamentally, whilst some of the current role constructs will continue, an overt focus on task will encourage people to highlight the ones (likely to be maintenance tasks) that do not fit in anyone's self image. At this stage, it becomes obvious that everyone looking to contribute to the communal effort will need to pay attention to the completion of these tasks. In fact, the communal infrastructure of pigs and chickens should go a long way to reassure anyone worried that some tasks will be left behind.

It is crucial to understand that, in mass collaboration, the leader's time is better spent helping individuals find the opportunities to reinforce their self-image whilst preventing the organizational roles derailing their strengths. The reality is that no one who truly loves what they do will ever reject the accountabilities necessary for their commitment to the company's success and sustainability. And, in true stereotypical French fashion, love is where we go to next to end our journey through these turbulent times.

The 30 second recap

We use two types of roles to define what we are accountable for. There are the roles created by the organization for the fulfilment of its purpose and the roles individuals build for themselves to gain fulfilment in their lives. As a result of the four trends, the organizational role we need to be fulfilled and the social role individuals want to fulfil (ie the source of engagement) become conflicted.

To be effective, leaders will need to help participants relate the tasks they need fulfilled to their self-image rather than create ever more sophisticated roles for them to embrace. Whilst organizations will still need to define roles in order to break the creation process into manageable and economical blocks, leaders will need to use a process of dialogue to help participants reinforce their self-image through the completion of these necessary tasks.

Notes

1   Data obtained from SETI@home website, Current Total Statistics page, last updated 13 January 2008.

2   Eugenie Samuel Reich (2004) Mysterious signals from light years away, *New Scientist*, 1 September.

3   Eugenie Samuel Reich (2004) Mysterious signals from light years away, *New Scientist*, 1 September.

4   Amir Alexander (2008) From SETI@home to Hominid Fossils: Citizen Cyberscience Reshapes Research Landscape, *SETI@home Update*, 15 January.

5   The clickworker project was born out of the realization that only a minimal proportion (about 20 per cent) of all data gathered on scientific missions are ever used. The Mars Global Surveyor generated some 25,000 images in its five-year mission. The clickworker programme was put in place to ensure these images would be fully capitalized upon.

6   For a more detailed comparison of the efforts of clickworkers against those of trained scientists you can visit http://clickworkers.arc.nasa.gov/documents/crater-marking.pdf.

7   Study by the Department of Information and Computer Science, University of California, Irvine.

11 Shift 4 – from money to love

In the late nineties, Daniel Goleman published a book that would popularize the term 'emotional intelligence'. The basic premise of emotional intelligence is that to be successful leaders need to both understand and manage their emotions so as not to derail their intent. Having had the chance to work alongside the team whose research would eventually lead to Goleman's second volume, *Working with Emotional Intelligence,* I remember debating whether the word 'emotion' would ever enter the corporate dictionary. So if business leaders would find it hard to embrace the word emotion, then brave (or foolish) is the business author who puts the word 'love' in the title of his or her book. Would business leaders ever be ready for the ultimate emotion – love?

Ready or not, Tim Sanders was willing to take on the fight. In 2002 he released his first book and boldly entitled it *Love is the Killer App.* And it seemed business was ready for love. *Love is the Killer App* made the *New York Times* bestseller list and Tim made the big time. In what is, as far as I am concerned, one of the most powerful 'how to' books for leaders, he argues that business success depends on three key factors: knowledge, networking and compassion. He goes on to show how, by becoming 'lovecats' (sharing knowledge, becoming a business matchmaker and building people up), anyone can achieve the impossible.

The assault of love on the corporate consciousness didn't stop with Tim. The first decade of the new millennium seemed to be a fruitful ground for the growth of the idea that business and love weren't mutually exclusive. The year 2005 gave us 'Lovemarks', the new marketing technique introduced to the world by charismatic Worldwide CEO of Saatchi & Saatchi, Kevin Roberts. Following Tim's example, he introduced another three-dimensional model, suggesting that by using Mystery (ie great inspiring stories), Sensuality (appealing to all the senses) and Intimacy (showing empathy and passion) organizations can do something that fads and brands can never sustain – command both respect and love. Granted it took Saatchi & Saatchi producing a series of groundbreaking films as part of a US$430 million contract that helped reposition JC Penney's brand before Kevin's 'Lovemark' idea was taken seriously. But the book eventually left its own 'Lovemark' on the business landscape.

The L word, so often heard in the dot com 1990s, so successfully used by Tim when he was still Chief Solutions Officer at Yahoo, and so well marketed by marketing supremo Kevin, could have switched off many executives. But their timing was impeccable. At the same time as love was entering the business dictionary, executives were already investigating the issue of commitment. They knew that in turbulent times commitment underpinned organizational success. What makes anyone committed to the organizational cause is a question many HR and marketing professionals have pondered for some time. Answering it underpins an organization's ability to create. Making the answer compelling underpins a business's ability to trade. As much as we have tried to disguise it, our answer has been painfully predictable: money. In social engagement terms this answer will no longer suffice.

The debate about the role of money in business has indeed become painful. It seems that anyone arguing that human motivation is too complex to be reduced purely to money always prefaces their argument by saying 'Of course, I am not saying money does not matter', thereby swiftly prompting their audience to switch off and carry on with their work. The proponents of money as a motivator, on the other hand, put themselves firmly in the pragmatist camp (a well-rewarded behaviour in most businesses), suggesting that, 'Of course things are more complicated but let's not kid ourselves that the quickest way to create commitment is still money'. It is a painful debate because it is a false debate. As we saw in Chapter 6, what ultimately determines any business's success is not the provision of a powerful answer to the question 'Why should I do what you want me to do?' but rather an ability to ensure the question never arises. When we have a simple, well-articulated narrative, supported by a focus on tasks, everyone is clear about how to achieve the purpose that drew the community together.

There are only two occasions when the question 'Why should I do what you want me to do?' might arise. The first is when the purpose of the endeavour is not in line with the purpose of the customer or the employee (ie social engagement is not possible). In these circumstances you may buy effort but you will never gain commitment (ie at least one of the parties involved doesn't want a relationship). The second is when the task is not seen to be in line with the implied purpose (ie there is no narrative linking task participation to purpose realization). In this case, a monetary reward might cover the cracks and make someone perform, but it will not buy their commitment either.

Before we go any further, let me be clear about what I think most businesspeople mean when they say they want commitment – and what I mean by commitment in the context of social engagement. When leaders ask for commitment, what they are asking for is devotion to the organization. They look for people who will join the organization with the aim of staying and caring enough about it to ensure that their contribution is maximized. Commitment is about putting the organization first. In practice, it means staying as long and working as hard as is needed for a task to be accomplished. It means showing flexibility to take any extra steps, whether planned or not, to ensure expectations are exceeded. Underlying these demands are two distinct ideas I use to define commitment.

The first is that commitment is about making a pledge to conduct a specific undertaking. Being committed, whether in our private or in our work lives, is about showing dedication. To be real, a commitment needs to be made.

The second idea underpinning the notion of commitment is the idea of obligation. A commitment is a felt obligation to do something, irrespective of how much we may want to do something else. This is a critical idea as it leads to the sustainability of the relationship (ie it would otherwise be nonsensical to talk about commitment) and highlights the fact that commitment and engagement go hand in hand. For commitment to exist both parties have to willingly relinquish some of their freedom to act.

What is clear, whilst not always remembered, is that the ideas under-pinning commitment are in fact the same whether in a work context or outside this. This is important, as many of the decisions we see as being appropriate when seeking to establish commitment at work would stand little scrutiny if exercised in a non-work relationship. Few personal relationships would survive intact an end-of-year appraisal designed to determine how much effort will be given over the coming year! Commitment is emotional whilst organizations rely on policy to underpin relationships. However much we might like to disguise it, the prime factor in, at least starting, a relationship between an individual (be they a customer or an employee) and an organization is money (in the form of price for the former and salary for the latter). So does money buy commitment? To find out, let's look at the kind of circumstances where money is a key factor.

Let's choose the financial services sector, or sales roles in any sector where there is a clear line of sight between performance obtained and reward gained.[1] In these roles, money underpins the contractual relationship. Typically the reward package will contain two parts. One is the salary paid to the individual, which, whilst it may be high in comparison to many other people's salaries, in fact forms the smallest part of the package. The largest part is the variable element attached to a number of targets to be met. There is an inherent simplicity to this package. You will get paid if you fulfil expectations and you risk your job if you don't. The difference between achievement and failure can run into millions of dollars. These situations are extreme indeed but they are helpful to us as they help us contrast them with the communities we have looked at so far, where money does not feature. So what can we learn from these cases in terms of commitment?

The first lesson is that money alone does not buy you commitment. Now, arguably, leaders looking to fill these roles are not necessarily looking for commitment. When you pay incentive plans running into the millions you are buying a certain kind of performance. You are buying a name and a track record. Executives talk about recruiting 'rain makers' or 'masters of the universe' in the hope that the new employee's name will be the brand that will attract clients. In this case, money might make sense as a tool for the strategy you are pursuing. The narrative is clear and seldom mentions commitment on either side. But can money actually deliver commitment?

The payment of the reward is directly related to the achievement of objectives, and not achieving the objectives leads to the loss of the position (ie the end of the relationship). In these cases, the relationship is purely contractual. Money buys you certain behaviours and buys you performance. It does not, however, buy you commitment. I mentioned earlier how, given that the definition of commitment is the same whether inside or outside the work context, we can judge the effectiveness of our commitment strategy by examining it under each realm. It is easy to see how a personal relationship based on money alone is not a recipe for commitment.

Outside organizations the idea of commitment put alongside money is nonsensical. The behaviour you have bought may feel like commitment, it may even look like commitment, but when tested, it is anything but commitment. Sure, the relationship can be sustainable provided the money doesn't run out or a better offer doesn't arise, but it is convenient rather than committed. Granted, with some skills on the part of one of the parties to the relationship and gullibility on the part of the other party, money can give you the illusion of love. But when the financial contract is removed the only outcome is one of the parties being poorer and the other one lonely. The Beatles were right – money can't buy you love. The fact that money does not buy commitment is clear to anyone who stops for long enough to assess the nature of human affairs.

But even if money does not buy commitment, far be it from me to say that it does not motivate if, by motivate, we mean encourage certain behaviours. I personally have always found being paid to be a great incentive to actually delivering a service, so I can vouch for money's effectiveness in that regard. However, the relationship between money and motivation is not as straightforward as it first seems. The second lesson from looking at extremely salary-geared jobs is that money is not actually the prime motivator. Money is a currency for motivation, not the motivation itself.

Let's go back to our 'rain makers'. Are they really money obsessed? Yes they are. Does that mean they are motivated by money? No it doesn't. Money is the currency that helps them purchase their motivation. Think about it this way. Maybe they are motivated by being the best at what they do – being number one. Maybe they are motivated by having a big house and a fast car. Maybe they are motivated by the need to keep their family financially secure. Regardless of what motivates them, money is a means to provide it, not an end in itself. It is as easy to forget as it is easy to observe in the thick of the action on the trading floor or when closing a big deal – that motivation does not reside in money. But if that is true, why the conventional organizational wisdom that money lies at the core of motivation?

The reason we rightly afford a motivational value to money is simply because its extrinsic motivational value is easier to manage than the complex intrinsic motivation of individuals. Money is highly effective in providing credible feedback for individuals looking to measure their achievement (which tends to be, if not the individual's main motivator, at least the value the organization encourages and rewards). In an environment where the achievement of targets makes the difference between satisfying your intrinsic motivational needs or not, money becomes a highly sought-after currency. Given that we can easily manipulate the extrinsic motivation and successfully achieve a given outcome to the satisfaction of both parties, it is no surprise that we see it as effective.

So, in those circumstances isn't the distinction between extrinsic and intrinsic motivation only the kind of pedantic hair-splitting question psychologists with too much time on their hands and few immediate problems to solve care about? Does it actually matter? Not really, if all you are trying to do is purchase performance. After all, who cares why money matters to people as long as it does. But if you are looking for commitment then suddenly the motivation of the individual plays a larger role. Remember, the idea of commitment is underpinned by moral obligation and pledge. To get both is why motivation matters. That leads us to what is arguably the third and most important lesson we can learn when looking at money-intensive environments. Money destroys the moral obligation at the heart of commitment.

Let's recap how we got here before we tackle that last point. So far we know that money does encourage certain kinds of desirable behaviours, but when it comes to creating commitment, money is far from being the most efficient tool at our disposal. But let's be fair, most organizations and their leaders understand that and, as a result, try to build social norms that will replicate the sense of obligation many have towards a community. We figure that by encouraging employees and customers to view the organization as a company we will get more of their discretionary effort and spend than if we work through contractual obligations. The fact that these efforts invariably lead to a narrative breakdown (why if you want commitment do you always reinforce the contract?) seems to escape us. Here is why.

In their seminal piece of research,[2] published under the title 'A fine is a price', Uri Gneezy from the University of Chicago and Aldo Rustichini from the University of Minnesota highlight what I call the narrative breakdown of money. The hypothesis they set out was that a system of fines could change the behaviour of people over time. Call it a negative incentive if you will but it's an incentive nevertheless. Here is a scenario that might be familiar to you.

It's your last meeting of the day and you know you will be cutting it fine to pick up your child at the day-care centre. You know you're going to have to chair the meeting in a masterly fashion if you are to finish in time for your train so you get everyone together and hope for the best. Halfway through the meeting, someone presents a new idea. You hadn't thought about it before, and let's face it, it's a brilliant idea. The conversation is intense and the promise of the new idea is amazing. Thoughts of chairing the meeting have gone out of your head and before you know it, you realize you have missed your train. You call the meeting to an end, pack up the laptop and run for the next train.

At the day-care centre, the last room has been closed and the lights have been switched off. Your child is now in the lobby, being looked after by an assistant who has agreed to stay behind. You come in flustered, late and apologetic. That day-care centre is worth its weight in gold to you. You know they won't let you down. Your child smiles, you smile, the teaching assistant doesn't. It's the second time in a month you're late.

Of course, twice is bad enough, but imagine being the owner of the day-care centre. With one hundred children to look after, late parents are beginning to cost you money. You need to pay overtime for the assistant left behind. Having been pushed over the limit by these inconsiderate parents you decide you are going to introduce a fine system. If parents are late, from now on they will have to pay. Now get back into your role as parent.

When you receive the newsletter introducing the fine system you aren't best pleased (after all you are only late in exceptional circumstances) but, being in business yourself, you understand the owner's intent and swear to yourself you will do better on your timekeeping. A month goes by and you stick to your promise. Everyone is happy. A week later, you know you shouldn't have, but you couldn't avoid it – you have booked another late meeting. And guess what, the bright idea of some weeks ago has now become a project and things aren't going smoothly. You get the status update and go into crisis-solving mode. You talk about options. Your occasional glances at the clock tell you that you're cutting it fine. What's going on in your head? Are you going to wrap up the meeting? After all, there is now an economic incentive encouraging you to do so. But this project is worth a lot of money to you – even, maybe, a promotion. You are a business executive so you ask yourself a business question.

Is the fine I am going to pay the day-care centre owner worth the money I am standing to make for my business? Assuming everything else stays the same (ie your child will not suffer irreparable trauma or the day-care centre is not going to expel your child) you decide to stay.

The incentive has had the exact opposite effect to the one anticipated by the day-care centre owner. As opposed to making sure parents arrive on time, a lot of parents have now taken the view you have taken. In fact, many now welcome the convenience they now take for granted. The owner who wanted to cut down on parents being late has now effectively increased the centre's opening hours. This wasn't meant to happen but in the experiment conducted by Uri Gneezy and Aldo Rustichini it did just that. What is going on? You may well point out to a badly designed incentive system. You may argue that if the penalty was exorbitant, parents would not risk this (conveniently forgetting that if the death penalty worked, at least 70 countries on Earth would be crime-free).

When we have been thinking about commitment, I have made the point that we seem to live in two separate universes – the work universe and the life universe. In the work universe resides an economic language where economic incentives rule. This is the universe of contractual obligations – the world of financial incentives and rewards. It is the world that we have used in organizations. It is a world where you weigh the pros and cons of a behaviour in relation to its financial impact (after all, money does affect behaviour). But as human beings, we also operate in a social domain full of social incentives and obligations. This is the world of morality and relationships. It's a world where you feel guilty and swear you'll never be late again.

What the owner has done by appealing to an economic incentive is to jump from one universe to the other at warp speed. By making it an economic rather than a social or moral punishment, the day-care centre owner has encouraged you to manage the situation rather than your emotions.

The problem for us is that commitment, because of the concepts of obligation and pledge that underpin it, inhabits a human, not an organizational universe. And whilst these two domains operate in parallel, their paths seldom cross. Economic incentives work against social ones and commitment suffers.

So, here we are. We now have three lessons from the world of money. We now know that money alone does not buy commitment. We recognize that money is not a prime motivator and that, indeed, it can destroy the very social and moral obligations we seek to introduce. But what can we learn from the world we have looked at so far in this book? In the communities I have described money plays a negligible part. I grant you that there might be some side financial benefits to belonging to one of these communities. Maybe being a master at Wikipedia might get you invited to share a few platforms on the lucrative conference circuit, or being a participant in SETI@home might enable you to write a few, paid for, articles in a magazine, but even that tends to be reserved for the platform owners. It is also true that a few of the million bloggers out on the web are managing to support their habit through online donations and click-through advertising, but for every one of them who makes a living out of the blog there are thousands who don't. So by and large, here we have a world devoid of direct financial incentives. What can we learn about commitment in that world? There are two lessons for us to take on board.

The first is that, whatever motivates an individual, it is their love for the community that provides this motivation. Right from the start, in Chapter 6, it became apparent that the very make-up of the community is an intricate system of social relationships based on reciprocity. The masters derive motivation from the dependents' use of the community for example. As with our organizations, there are a myriad of intrinsic motivational factors at play inside the actors of the community. They may look for self-aggrandizement by being masters. Participants may enjoy the social dynamics and the relationships the company provides. Dependents may get immense satisfaction from belonging to new, innovative and groundbreaking projects. Whatever the intrinsic motivation, love is the currency (the extrinsic motivation) in achieving it. For commitment to exist the people involved have to love what they do. So what do I mean by love?

In his bestselling and best-known book *The Road Less Travelled,* US psychiatrist Morgan Scott Peck defines true love (as opposed to some romantic notion of dependent love, which he considers to be a myth) as being about our ability to value, nurture and help other people grow. It is not about us being some kind of teacher or being 'in charge' of others. It is our acceptance that making others stronger makes us stronger too. The recognition that together we are interdependent. In Peck's definition, love is not just a nice feeling, it is hard work.

This interdependence defines the very nature of the communities we have looked at. It is the foundation on which moral and social obligations rest. What is critical is the recognition that this kind of interdependence cannot be bought. The only way it exists is if it is driven out of a sense that love is in fact critical to all involved (ie I cannot fake it in the hope that I will create interdependence as interdependence only matters if I have love). And this leads us to the second important finding – commitment only arises when all parties are in love.

Few would argue that a relationship is healthy when one party decides to ignore their own needs in order to bolster the needs of the other. Even fewer would advance that a loving relationship is possible when one party does not share that love, and hopefully no one would ever suggest that unrequited love leads to a higher state of consciousness (unless they are keen to advance the cause of poets of the romantic age). Because a community can only survive if the intricate system of relationships that underpins it is thriving, when one party falls out of love, the other suffers. If masters decide that they no longer care for the needs of participants or dependents, the community will ultimately descend into chaos, confusion and in-fighting (which, to a lesser extent, is what we witnessed when looking at Wikipedia's growth). Someone's contribution will only happen if that person is in love with what they do, who they are doing it for and with, and feel loved as a result.

But business still isn't that kind of community. In most organizations, money is and will always be a large part of the equation. So how can we reconcile both the financial and the social incentives? Here again it is not so much about leaders having new tools at their disposal but, once again, more about how they must shift their focus and attention.

eBay is a good example of a hybrid organization and company. On the one hand eBay is a giant business home to businesses of all sizes. It serves the full range, from individuals looking to sell some of their unwanted junk to businesses looking to sell their wares, from customers looking to bag a few bargains to businesses buying cheap supplies.

eBay as an organization follows a pretty traditional, hierarchical topology, as do many of the businesses it hosts. On the other hand, it is a thriving community of volunteers with a topology similar to the other communities we have looked at. Visiting its online forum will help you quickly identify its masters. A look at the frequently-asked questions forum will help you see the participants. A few hours spent digging behind the scenes might even help you spot a few Ducks. This hybrid model helps us understand how economic and social incentives can coexist.

eBay knows that little can be done by the organization without first generating input from the community. Executives know that the community is the linchpin of their success. They understand that their marketing efforts have been largely superseded by those of the community. Looking inside eBay (or any other online community-driven business for that matter) will help you see the areas leaders must focus on.

Earlier in this chapter, I noted how commitment is emotional whilst organizations rely on policy to underpin relationships. Creating real commitment (as opposed to mimicking behaviours that feel like it) needs us to look beyond a policy framework. HR policies should not drive leadership focus. Let policies take care of the economic incentives and ensure you nurture the social incentive. Minimize the narrative breakdowns by focusing on the community and amplifying simplicity (remembering that whilst money sits in the camp of simplification, it is the enemy of coherence). Focusing on what matters for the creation of commitment means doing two things.

The first is to ensure that you love what you do. There is little that is more destructive than professing love when it isn't felt, or asking for love without being prepared to give it. Whether intended or not, eBay has been caught a few times introducing policies (mainly focused on revenue) that the community has taken as lack of care for their work. There is nothing wrong with the business having to survive (all those who rely on it for their existence are not stupid enough to wish its death); however, the relationship between the organization and the community is symbiotic – neither can drive the other. The key for leaders is to remember that without a genuine love for the community they work in they can never expect commitment to be given.

This means, as eBay has found out, endless debates and discussions that provide encouragement and reassurance and sometimes the inevitable fight that provides relief. A relationship is healthier and more likely to engender commitment when both parties acknowledge their fears, frustrations and needs. Too often I find myself talking to leaders who are tired, disillusioned and on the verge of leaving an organization, whilst at the same time trying to put on a show of asking for passion and commitment from others. The alternative route of honesty, reciprocity and trust is indeed 'a road less travelled' but it is also one that forges the respect on which commitment thrives.

The second thing leaders have to focus on is the fact that social incentives can be created by focusing on the community rather than the individual. This can be a counter-intuitive idea for leaders who for years have been told that they not only need to know what motivates their followers, but they need to appeal to these motives.

It is true that in the business world, just like in the real world, most of us get to impact only those people in our immediate sphere of influence. But our constant focus on the individual has been to the detriment of social incentives. Our obsession with engineering each piece to perfection has meant that we have taken our eye off the bigger picture of our purpose. The role of the leader is to make the community stronger so the individual can find themselves in it. Think about the eBay business.

Of course, it is possible with the technological advances in place for any executive at eBay to know a lot about any of the community members. They might even seek their opinion in order to improve the business. But where they add the most value is using all these insights to build a stronger community rather than spending their time convincing host business owners that they really ought to be motivated by one particular function over another. This focus on individuals has a tendency to lead to a contractual rather than a social obligation.

Of course, whilst in the idealized world of a business book these things can sound rather simple, none of them are easy to do. It is a whole lot easier to operate in one clear communal narrative or one simple business one, rather than in a world spanning the two. The truth is, however, our world has always been spanning the two. The fact that changes have helped us realize that things don't have to be the way they have always been doesn't mean we never wanted something better. The reality that the emancipation brought about by modern business practices has had the effect of making us wish for simpler, more social times is not to be feared as a newfangled demand. Making the transition is not easy but we have a pretty good guide to help us navigate. Ladies and gentlemen, Elvis is in the building.

The 30 second recap

In the long run, commitment is crucial to leaders. To get it, they are willing to pay for it. But commitment cannot be bought. To secure it, leaders must look at their organizations through two new, non-financial lenses.

The first is to realize that both parties involved in the relationship have to love what they do. To be successful the organization needs all involved to embrace their task and identify themselves with the narrative.

The second is that a social rather than economic incentive can be created by focusing on the community rather than the individual. For leaders this may be somewhat counter-intuitive as we have been told as leaders that we need to understand what motivates an individual and focus our efforts on maximizing that motivation. But what matters to the functioning of our communities is not what motivates individuals but rather that they direct that motivation to making the community stronger.

Notes

1   I know many will point out the collapse of financial systems across the world as proof that there is little to no correlation between shareholder value and executive. But I am here talking about the setting of highly measurable objectives and the payments arising from them rather than looking at whether these objectives (or indeed the legitimacy of the means used to obtain them) are the right ones.

2   Uri Gneezy and Aldo Rustichini (2000) A fine is a price, *Journal of Legal Studies*, **29** (1), pp 1–17. This piece of research has entered the realm of everyday business having been talked about in *Freakonomics* and *Predictably Irrational*, two business bestsellers. Readers of my first book *The Connected Leader* might also recognize the parallels between their research and my own failed experience of using incentives to reinforce behaviour with my daughter, Charlotte.

12 The Elvis fallacy

On 25 April 2007, 30 years after he reportedly left the building, Elvis made a very public comeback. The original idol lent his services to the *American Idol* television show by making a special appearance alongside Celine Dion. Together they sang his hit song 'If I Can Dream'. But the audience wasn't dreaming; it really was the real dead Elvis performing live due to the magic of technology. But this was the second time Elvis had made a comeback in the first decade of our new millennium.

In 2002, Junkie XL remixed a song first recorded by Elvis Presley in 1968 and used in one of his movies, *Live a Little, Love a Little*. The single went straight to number 1 in over 20 countries. 'A Little Less Conversation' became an anthem that could not be ignored. It was used in the soundtracks of movies from *Bruce Almighty* to *Ocean's 13*, via *Lilo and Stitch, Jackass Two* and *Shark Tale*.

It also became a favourite line for journalists and commentators to use every time they were dissatisfied. Politicians of all persuasions were asked for 'a little less conversation and a little more action'. Executives spanning the entire economic spectrum from the health to the financial sectors were directed to have 'a little less conversation and take a little more action'. In fact, a quick search on Google will show you how often and broadly the song title was used as a shorthand by journalists and commentators (proving once and for all that, when it comes to headline writing, our imagination is as limited as our ability to jump on a bandwagon is great).

But if journalists saw the resurgence of the song as an opportunity to capitalize temporarily on its popularity, business leaders should have recognized it as the best articulation of one of their most entrenched and mistaken beliefs – actions speak louder than words.

That executives have harboured that belief is not surprising – transactional involvement is built on actions. Create clarity, communicate a plan, hold people accountable and reward appropriate outcomes. The sequential nature of the process reinforces the belief that doing something to others is the one sure way to success. On the other hand, social engagement, as we have seen, is not a sequential process. Simplicity, narratives, tasks and love reinforce each other. So, at the very least, the 'doing' part of leadership needs to be more complex, more refined, more interconnected and holistic. But the fallacy that organizations suffer from a 'little too much conversation and not enough action syndrome' does not simply rest on misguided beliefs about the type of actions to take. It is born out of a failure to accept that words and actions are in fact intrinsically linked. There are two important aspects to this.

The first is that words can pretty much predict the nature of the actions likely to be taken. Consider the following. If the eyes are a window to the soul then the written word is the vista to emotions. Every day, evidence shows us clearly how words are a good way of judging someone's mental and physical state of health. If I tell you I feel depressed and tired, you don't need to be a doctor (or indeed a mind reader) to know that I might not be on top form. But what about if I don't tell you how I feel? Can you still guess from the words I use when discussing a topic totally unrelated to my health how I am? James W Pennebaker, Roger J Booth and Martha E Francis think you can and they can even help you out.

Drawing on decades of research and studies into the correlation between words used and physical and mental health, James, Roger and Martha have devised a way of finding out how to read our health. They call this Linguistic Inquiry and Word Count (LIWC).[1] LIWC is a piece of software that sorts the types of words used in a text into a dozen categories (eg social words, big words, self references etc) to assess a person's health. For example when people feel good, they tend to rely less on the use of first person pronouns. The team have analysed the words of many famous and infamous people.

They have looked at the words of McCartney and Lennon and put the transcripts of the presidential election debates between Senators Obama and McCain through the software. They have even found that whilst Osama Bin Laden's words show little change over time, those uttered by his 'lieutenant', Al Ayman al-Zawahri, show growing feelings of insecurity.[2] Whilst I am yet to analyse this book for fear of what it might reveal, the idea that we can, literally, *read* someone is not that far-fetched for self- and socially-aware leaders.

We know that our moods are contagious. We can feel how the atmosphere in our workplace changes as the mood changes. This happens because of the words we use and the attitude we display. Clearly our words and our actions, and by extension the actions of others, are not disconnected in the way conventional managerial wisdom would have it. Words speak at least as loudly as actions.

The second element we need to consider to put the fallacy to rest is our belief that actions and conversations exist on two separate continua. Whilst I have always been fond of the saying 'When all is said and done, more is usually said than done', not least for the cleverness of the turn of phrase, it does not hold up to scrutiny. The fact is that there cannot be efficient actions without effective conversations.

For the last two years I have been conducting a small experiment. Whilst I am loath to tell you about it for fear of never again being able to use it as an energizing start to a speech, the result is telling. Every time I have been asked to speak at a conference I have started by giving the audience the same test, and irrespective of which country, continent, industry, audience profile and seniority, the results have always been the same.

The test is a simple arithmetic test. Participants are asked to complete simple additions, multiplications, subtractions and divisions. There are never more than two digits in any one number. I tell participants that whilst the test is not difficult (pointing out that my daughter Charlotte, at 10, has no problems completing it), there is a complication. I go on to explain that the test is made more difficult because I will not tell them how long they have to complete it. I close by giving them the instructions to complete as many right calculations correctly as they can, as quickly as they can.

As soon as I utter the word 'go', participants rush to complete the task. Even though none of them know my daughter you can tell all of them want to beat her. The little voice in their head is telling them 'Go on, if a 10-year-old can do it, show him how you can do it better and quicker than her'. You may see this as a sad indictment of our mental state in organizations, where grown-ups can't bear to lose to a 10-year-old, but this ability to take decisive and fast actions is also what has made these people the successful executives they are.

By the time I end the test (no more than minutes) a pattern emerges. Most people will have done about 20 calculations out of the 40 possible. A few will have done more and a few less. As you would anticipate, the result is somewhat of a bell curve. But invariably about a tenth (at most) of the audience will have done a lot less than the rest and obtained a completely different set of results. When I call out the answers, the majority of people suddenly realize there must have been a trick they had not spotted. And, without fail, they realize that at the top of the page there are two lines of instructions that clearly state that 'In the following simple arithmetic problems, a plus (+) sign means to multiply, a divide (÷) sign means to add, a minus (−) sign means to divide, and a times (×) sign means to subtract. Complete the problems following these directions'.

The first reaction is, of course, to blame me! After all I said this was simple and there was no trick other than the challenge of time. I must have been lying. I point out that I gave them all the same instructions and that, to my mind, eight times two is no more difficult than eight plus two. You can feel the pride of the people who read the instructions. They know that leadership is not just about taking action, it is also about having sufficient self-control to read the instructions and understand the reality of the test. But that is not what makes this test so interesting.

What is interesting to me is that I have administered this simple test to thousands of people in groups ranging from 10 to 1,000 and never has anyone, having spotted the instructions, turned to the group and said, 'Watch out, there is a trick, make sure you read the instructions'. Even when the audience is from a single department in a single organization, social bonds disappear as fast as the excitement of the competition takes over. So why should such varied audiences be so similarly conditioned?

Most of our leadership behaviours are the results of the organization's valorization of our willingness to take action. The social systems reinforce and reward our ability to act fast under pressure. We learn to value that need to achieve to the point that its fulfilment delivers instant gratification. The more pressure is put on us, the more we look to satisfy our need to achieve. Organization processes are designed to appeal to that need. So when faced with a test, our drive takes over and, provided the task looks similar to tasks we have previously successfully completed (like an arithmetic test), we get to work. Whilst developing sufficient self-control to keep that drive in check long enough to read the instructions might be a good recipe for success, it is not sufficient in a world of 'leadershift'.

In that world success depends on fostering the communal links. In the case of our test this is about making sure that whoever spots the trick feels an obligation to share their finding (as opposed to pride in not sharing it in order to win a competition). It is telling that at no stage do I mention the word competition when giving out my instructions for the test, so why do they hear it?

We act on the basis of what we hear, not what is said. After all, even directives are words that give rise to actions and we all know that even the strongest directives may sometimes not be enacted. To ensure that this doesn't happen we look to make directives clearer and incentives (positive or negative) high. By doing so we forget the importance of conversations. Let me explain.

Imagine I am sitting at the dinner table with my children and George starts to put salt on his dinner. I realize that he seems to be putting on more salt than is necessary for taste or good for him. I could say 'George, could you stop putting salt on your plate please as you now have more than enough.' That's a directive and it may or may not be enacted (let's say for the sake of argument that it is). Alternatively I might also just say 'Oh George,' in a tone that conveys something is not quite right and George, being the clever boy he is, will quickly put two and two together and the salt down (we hope). In this latter example, George acts not on the actual meaning of the words, but on the meaning he attaches to the words. In another example, you may be too hot in your office but unable to reach the window. As I sit next to you, you ask 'Emmanuel, can you reach that window?' I will probably get up and open the window for you. Please note that at no stage did you ever ask for the window to be opened, but in my mind I hear your request.

So whilst I never intended the mathematical test to be a competition, participants clearly assume I did. This is what linguists call an indirect speech act.[3] We act on the basis of the meaning we ascribe to words as well as the actual meaning. That ascribed meaning is the result of our personal history and shared experiences. I open the window because I know that when you ask me if I can reach something it is usually because you want it and can't reach it. George puts the salt down because he knows that 'Oh George,' is shorthand for 'Stop whatever you're doing and act surprised'!

So, regardless of what Elvis would have us believe, conversations and actions are intrinsically linked. Effective actions happen as a result of shared assumptions and a sense of shared history. The only way we can build these common reference points is through effective conversations.

The fact that instructions may be misconstrued or directives misinterpreted rests more on the absence of that shared history (ie we do not understand the demands) rather than a badly expressed directive. So whilst clearer directives may increase the likelihood of something getting done, unfortunately they need to frame the requirement so tightly that conversation is impossible. As a result a vicious cycle ensues as the lack of conversation limits shared history, which in turn will require tighter future directives. Eventually the potential for social engagement disappears and we are back in transactional involvement (the very thing that the trends are making ineffective).

Embracing the idea that conversations are the only effective and efficient route towards effective actions is critical to achieving success in the new world created by the DEAD trends. This is why understanding and eradicating the Elvis fallacy is so critical in achieving success in a post-DEAD trend world.

So far I have looked at the world of business under two headings – organizations and companies. The first heading is a shorthand for hierarchically structured (in terms of roles) organizations as we know them today (whilst acknowledging that the hierarchy itself will always play a more or less pronounced part in the culture of the workplace). The second is my way to describe a network of relationships with a non-hierarchical (in terms of roles, but in many ways no less organized in terms of activities) community. For their success, both of these rely on the ability to secure engagement, alignment, accountabilities and commitment on the part of participants.

I have argued that the way we obtain engagement, alignment, account-ability and commitment will need to change as a result of the pressure put on our organizations. So the methods we use must differ widely as we move from the organization's transactional involvement to the company's social engagement model. We will need to go from clarity, plans, roles and money to simplicity, narrative, tasks and love.

In my first book, *The Connected Leader*, I argued that organizations were, in fact, formal processes that relied on social networks for their energy. I made the point that leaders needed to connect to these networks through trust, align their energy to the delivery of formal objectives by providing purpose and maintain that alignment through dialogue. In many ways this book is a prequel to *The Connected Leader*. The recipe above is the way in which leaders can achieve the change from a pre- to a post-DEAD trend world.

But when the reach of the social networks extends beyond the boundaries of the formal organization the role of conversations becomes even more important. Companies are not organizations. They rely on a broader set of actors than can be found inside their formal boundaries. The distinctions between old and new, expert and novice, involved and committed or customer and employee blur as a result of the four trends. Involving an entire community in an act of dialogue becomes critical. Let me give you a clear example of what this looks like in a 'real' business.

If a start-up is a place full of energy, passion, dedication to a cause and a boundless enthusiasm to achieve, then Rabobank is the oldest of all the start-ups I have come across. I call this Dutch cooperative bank a 100-year-old start-up. Walking around the bank's central office in Utrecht feels like walking around any garage in Silicon Valley. Granted it's a big garage with thousands of people in it, but it feels like a place of opportunity.

Rabobank is one of the few real cooperative banks in Europe.[4] It represents the coming together of local Dutch banks who found strength in numbers. Like all start-ups Rabobank owes its existence to what we would now call a gap in the market and what, 100 years ago, they called a void needing to be filled. That void was the inability of farmers to get credit. The lack of steady income streams and the hazards of working the earth made it hard for anyone involved in agriculture to secure loans. In 19th-century Europe many local agricultural cooperatives formed to fill that void.

Local Dutch cooperatives adopted five principles of business. The first was the joint liability of their members, which ensured a cohesive community. The second was the management of their processes by unpaid volunteers designed to minimize administration costs. The third was the reserving of profits to ensure the banks' sustainability. The fourth was the contained geographical reach of local branches to keep close to their core base. Finally, the fifth and last was the autonomy of the local membership to keep the business grounded. Eventually these local businesses would come together under one umbrella to enable them to coordinate and minimize their running costs.

In the mid-1990s, at a time when most banks were looking at organizational and governance structures that would maximize their freedom to act and ability to take risks, Rabobank staged one of the biggest conversations of its existence with its stakeholders. There were two key questions to answer. Is our cooperative structure right for the future and, if so, what do we need to do to re-energize our membership? Stakeholders answered a resounding yes to the first part of the question and the bank has focused much of its time since then working on the three levers that would once again make it a thriving community – interests, involvement and management. The void Rabobank had looked to fill had been filled and it needed a refreshed purpose for its existence. They found that purpose in the pressing need of our times to address some of the challenges of global agricultural and food businesses, as well as advances in technological solutions to our environmental and climate crisis.

I have been lucky to meet many people who work for Rabobank. All share one characteristic that many leaders say they value in their people, but would probably and understandably prefer they didn't experience in practice. Rabobank people are questioning people. They question everything. They discuss any idea or concept you put their way. They think frustratingly deeply about whatever issue is at hand. I experienced that frustration firsthand as I debated at length the idea of advantages and disadvantages of cooperative structures with them. Whatever we seemed to be agreeing on, someone would point out a flaw and start the conversation all over again.

I put that frustration to the executives I met at Rabobank Group, when we met to discuss leadership. I wanted to know how they coped with having their ideas seemingly challenged rather than effectively implemented. Their answer does more to destroy the Elvis fallacy than any writing of mine could do.

In most cases, executives know they will have to sell their ideas. But most of them know that the selling happens after the decision has been made. They normally will gather a team of advisers and colleagues to discuss options. They will make the decision, communicate it and look for it to be implemented whilst they continue to sell it. In Rabobank's case, however, the situation is different. As custodians of the cooperative spirit, leaders see their job as communicating ideas before a decision can be made. And they don't do this just to a team of colleagues, they need to do it to everyone from farmers to branch managers. Imagine, if you will, trying to get a cost-cutting exercise underway when most of the people who are likely to suffer from it need to sign on the dotted line first.

But Rabobank executives don't see this as a problem. In fact they very much see it as the strength of the bank. In their view executives who think their ideas will be implemented the minute they come up with them are deluding themselves. They know that even when a decision has been made you still need to get people on board. So even if you are able to issue an edict, the likelihood is that it will take weeks and months before it is enacted. If you take efficiency as being the shortest route from idea to implementation rather than decision to implementation, their way of working wins hands down. Why? Simply because by the time the decision is made everyone involved in its implementation is on board. The conversations have created the sense of ownership and buy-in as well as, in most cases, made the decision better than any edict could achieve.

What makes these executives able to cope with this is their ability to draw people into conversations. They don't have anything to prove. They have a point of view and are comfortable with their place in the world. So they cope with challenges not as personal attacks but as furthering the search for the best solution, which they do not automatically assume they have. At a time when banks are collapsing, Rabobank's cooperative essence has given it the checks and balances that have ensured it has stayed true to its purpose. It never swayed too far towards risk.

A few years ago many might have accused it of being boring. But if boring is keeping your AAA rating and tier 1 solvency ratio, attracting ever more retail customers looking for a safe home in order to lend to your stated cause of agriculture, food and environmental technology, then give me boring any day. As I look to the future, it is not hard to imagine that the cooperative system is the closest we will ever get to a DEAD trend-proof governance structure.

These insights I gained from Rabobank's executives on the roles of conversations in facilitating implementations reminded me of the findings of two consultants. In 1982 these two young McKinsey consultants were about to launch a publishing sensation, creating in the process the business book market as we know it today. *In Search of Excellence* was the start of many things, some good, some bad, some awesome and some downright scary. The meteoric rise of Tom Peters as a business guru with his trademark love of capital letters and exclamation marks was a good thing. The new-found focus on replicating best practice proved bad in the long run. The sudden popularization of the idea that business should be studied, thought about and professionalized was awesome. At the same time, the birth of a generation of copycat business writers who sought fame and fortune by uncovering correlations that they passed on as causations, rather than the opinions they really were, was downright scary. But *In Search of Excellence* also launched a very useful management practice.

Tom tells the story of rehearsing in his co-author Bob Waterman's hotel room prior to their appearance on the *Today* show.[5] They got into an argument as to who would get to mention, on national television, the practice they had grown to love the most out of all the ones they had uncovered. They couldn't agree so flipped a coin. Peters lost and regrets it to this day. There was something pretty cool about being the first one to talk about 'Management by Wandering About'. But, to Peters' regret, it was Waterman's appearance that catapulted MBWA into the business lexicon.

It became a fad overnight. The idea that by wandering around your business you could gather valuable information and impact motivation may have been common sense but certainly wasn't common then. Over time, many executives changed 'wandering' to 'walking', possibly fearing that wandering might sound a little too aimless to their shareholders. Most eventually abandoned the practice, preferring instead to have others come to them with a well-publicized, less time- and energy-consuming 'open-door policy'. Abandoning the practice had far-reaching consequences.

MBWA enabled executives to keep close to 'the troops' and understand the inner workings of their own organizations. Most executives know how hard it is to figure out what is and isn't real inside the numerous slide decks handed over to them by subordinates. The higher up you go in an organization, the more difficult it is to know what is really going on. They say the Queen of England must think the world outside Buckingham Palace smells strange as any building she visits has always been freshly painted. That's why executives quickly saw the good sense in adopting the practice. But whilst MBWA did indeed increase the chance a leader would have of confronting realities, it also had another advantage. This was one that had been known since the 17th century.

Like the proverbial Renaissance man, Herman Boerhaave was fascinated by numerous fields of human knowledge. In 17th-century Europe he was famous beyond his native Holland for his insights into physics and botany. But he was also a pioneer in anatomy and medicine, eventually becoming one of the fathers of modern medicine teaching. He would dissect a corpse in front of his students to pass on knowledge about anatomy but he also started a practice still in use today in all teaching hospitals – the grand rounds.

Grand rounds are a ritual of all medical teachings. A group of medics gather together to discuss a case and potential treatment. Anyone who has ever watched an episode of the *House MD* television series will be familiar with the back and forth discussions, arguments and counter arguments, challenges and guesses taking place in front of a whiteboard, all designed to get closer to the right answer. What we fail to understand, at our own risk, is that far from being just a tool leaders can use to confront reality, MBWA is the grand round of modern business. Communities grow and develop through the conversations that take place between their members. The result of these conversations are targeted, positive and profitable actions – the essence of the still elusive learning organization.

Leaders wanting to make their organizations DEAD trend-proof would do well therefore to think of themselves as facilitators of conversations. They have to achieve the difficult balance between providing a voice and a figurehead to a community looking to assemble behind a cause, and not being prominent enough to steal or appropriate that community's voice by assuming they are its sole embodiment. This requires maturity, confidence and assurance as well as humility, self-awareness and resolve.

Most of our conversations today are problem-solving conversations. We are so well versed in the art of problem solving that we have come to see organizations themselves as problems to be solved. Yet communities aren't problems. Organizations aren't problems. People are not problems. We would do well to remember to value our strengths rather than fixate on solving perceived problems. Of course issues will not need to be addressed, but we need to understand that solving issues only matters because we value the communities we seek to lead. If we genuinely believe that organizations are problems to be fixed we should start questioning our need for them. With that in mind, breaking the 'Elvis Fallacy' requires us to start by valuing what we have and, together, imagining and designing what we are imaginative enough to envisage. The idea that change starts with a negative – a 'burning platform' – is a warped belief that dismisses out of hand the power of humanity by starting from the point of view of deficiency. It has not served us well.

There are four steps that I believe will prove crucial in developing the strength and resilience leaders will need to foster simplicity, narratives, tasks and love in their organizations.

The first is to learn to do nothing. The focus of 'leadershift' is not on what to start or do but rather on what to stop. Leaders of communities are benevolent dictators whose role it is to act as arbiters when called upon to do so by the community, rather than active shapers of outcomes.

The second step is to contribute to the narrative. Narrative ownership is distributed through the system rather than owned by the leader, so

whilst it is legitimate (and recommended) for the leader to contribute, that contribution is in no way superior to the contribution of
others (unless made as a result of a demand on the leader by the
community).

The third is to build personal reputation. To be able to navigate through
the mass collaborative effort, leaders need to have a solid reputation
(ie earn the right to lead). Whilst reputation is underpinned by an
individual's behaviour and capabilities, it is ultimately accorded by
community members. This may seem rather Machiavellian to many
and a bit too much like marketing to others, but thinking about your
impact and managing your influence is a strength successful leaders
have.

Finally, the last step is one that I spoke about in the last chapter but is
so crucial that is worth repeating – learn to love what you do. The idea
that work must carry meaning is not that easy. Indeed searching for
meaning and purpose at work is more likely to leave one wanting and
depressed than energized. However, if we refocus away from role to
task and learn to embrace our strengths and passions rather than our
measured contribution it is likely that we will find more energy.

Mass participation is not to be feared, even as it challenges the very
essence of our models of value creation. It is a much more natural (and
therefore energizing) form of value creation than the one imposed
on us by our organizational models. This is probably why whenever
organizations fail, they do so because a merry band of amateurs have
become critical competitors by forming highly-tuned value-creation
communities. These are the communities that are charting our
future.

The 30 second recap

Conversations are the lifeblood of social engagement. Do not believe anyone who tells you that actions speak louder than words. They are wrong for two reasons.

First there cannot be any action without words. Even commands are words. The only way to secure engagement, alignment, accountability and commitment is to involve the community in a discussion on its direction.

Second, there cannot be effective and efficient actions without conversations. Issuing an order may give the impression of action but it is one-sided action. The person issuing it needs to accept the fact that it is only their view that will carry the day. This not only limits the potential for engagement but also slows down implementation as community members try to reconcile their view of the world with the directive issued.

The only way to sustain engagement is to accept that the leader's role is to help the community create its own story and history through a process of relating and conversing.

Notes

1   To learn more about LIWC visit http://www.liwc.net/liwcdescription. php, where you will find relevant information including, for the geeks amongst us, discussions on the psychometric validity of the method.

2   J Wapner (2008) He Counts Your Words (Even Those Pronouns), *New York Times*, 13 October.

3   Linguists amongst you may rightly point out that things are somewhat simplified in my explanation. For those concerned about getting detailed definitions or wanting more information, you may want to read *Speech Acts: An essay in the philosophy of language* by John R Searle, published in 1969 by Cambridge University Press.

4   Rabobank has a long, complex and fascinating history to which I cannot do justice in this book. If you want to know more, as well as paying its website a visit (www.rabobank.com) I have drawn from a book called *The Bank with a Difference – The Rabobank and cooperative banking*, published by the bank itself in 2002.

5   100 Ways to Succeed #11: MBWA Lives & Rules & Is Ubiquitous! in DISPATCHES from the NEW WORLD of WORK, www.tompeters. com.

Concluding thoughts

'What saves a man is to take a step. Then another step. It is always the same step, but you have to take it.'

Antoine de Saint-Exupéry (1939) *Wind, Sand and Stars*

To anyone interested in mass collaboration, 2005 was a seminal year. A band, unheard of by mainstream audiences and signed to a small independent label with little to no marketing support, found itself with a number one hit in the UK charts. But if the Arctic Monkeys became a famed case of mass collaboration in action, they also tell us something about the changing nature of leadership.

Since their formation in 2002, the Arctic Monkeys had only played in small venues to a small but loyal army of followers. Being unsigned, they decided to make demo CDs to distribute freely to their fans. They figured that if the fans had heard the songs before the gig they could sing along to the words, thereby making the atmosphere better. So when their followers started ripping and distributing bootleg copies they saw this as something to be encouraged, not feared. When those same devotees started a MySpace page the band's following increased. The web became the tool of choice for Arctic Monkeys enthusiasts eager to spread the word. Their devotion and relentless efforts encouraged more and more people to attend the gigs leading to the eventual signing of the band by a small independent label and then onto the chart success they've enjoyed since.

Many commentators have written about the importance of social network technology to promote ideas, products, brands and indeed bands. What was striking for me, however, was not the efforts of their fans – I had been studying mass collaboration for long enough not to be surprised any more by the power of crowds – rather, it was the band's role in all of this that interested me. Although clearly seen as leaders of the movement by their fans, the band had neither started nor controlled any of their efforts. The band members themselves have even commented on their lack of technological savvy, admitting that their use of the web seldom goes beyond sending e-mails. They were voted leaders without ever standing for election.

The Arctic Monkeys are an example of 'leadershift' in action, where the role of leaders is to create an environment people want to inhabit (helping them maintain Hardin's commons of Chapter 3) rather than sell a vision. In that way, the Arctic Monkeys are the music industry's Second Life. That kind of leadership is a step into the unknown for any of us, but it is nevertheless a step full of promises and possibilities.

The DEAD trends do *not*, in any way, diminish our yearning for leadership. We want to follow. We want to be inspired. We want to be led. This is not because we are weak or paralysed by fear, nor because of some deficiency that leaders need to fix. Instead, it is because we want someone to typify the changes we wish to make. We want someone to be the figurehead of a movement we want to drive.

In 2008 the United States of America found itself with a new president. Regardless of geographical location or political affiliation, no one can deny the historical nature of the landslide victory of the 44th President of the United States.

I started this book with a T-shirt so it seems appropriate to mention another one in these concluding thoughts. That T-shirt is one I saw worn by a woman, moved to tears, as she watched President Barack Obama cross the threshold of the Oval Office for the first time. It simply read 'Rosa Parks sat. Martin Luther King Junior marched. Barack Obama ran. All so our children could dream.'

Barack Obama's victory is a powerful reminder of our desire for leadership. Many have commented on his use of the internet and social networking technologies. Yet this wasn't the real breakthrough. Social networking technology has become pervasive because it facilitates rather than drives what we humans crave – social interactions. The real breakthrough of the Democratic candidate's campaign wasn't technology but using technology to facilitate community organizing on a grand scale.

Watching the campaign was like watching a lesson in 'leadershift'. Capitalizing on the promises of a generational trend, understanding the power of the expertise trend, harnessing rather than fearing the attention trend and rejoicing at the opportunities offered by the democratic trend gave the candidate an unprecedented momentum. When others looked for transactional involvement (ie getting votes) through segmentation, Barack Obama looked to build social engagement through communities (ie welcoming a tribe). It was no surprise that his first win during the primaries came at the Ohio caucuses. Caucuses are designed for communities. They thrive on volunteers and mass participation. His army of unpaid volunteers went on to replicate that success elsewhere.

His powerful rhetoric created simplicity. The message had been simplified not dumbed down. 'Yes we can' gave the movement coherence through communal values. Simplicity enabled people to engage.

There wasn't a home-made sign at any Obama rally. Every message, every sign, every e-mail, every site, every speech, every interview, every debate reinforced a narrative built on the hope change could bring rather than the fear it might create. 'Change we can believe in' was the narrative reinforced every step of the way.

The focus on roles was replaced by a focus on tasks. Anyone registering for e-mail updates from the campaign was left in no doubt about the tasks that needed to be fulfilled. 'We need a contribution of $5' was as likely to be asked as 'We need you to phone your friends'. Community organizing has always been about simple, defined tasks that contribute to the broader purpose.

But above all, it was love that carried the day – love for the image their candidate projected of themselves. This was love for a vision of the United States of America, love for a world people wanted to reconnect to, love for an ideal and an idea. That idea was that no matter where you are from, no matter what the colour of your skin is, no matter what the problems you face are, you too could be called upon to lead.

It is easy to be cynical about the American dream. In a world where the deck is still stacked firmly against the many to the advantage of the powerful few, it is easy to dismiss dreams. But dreams give us energy. They give us something to work towards. They give us courage and faith. With the election of Barack Obama, 'leadershift' won its first election and that seems like a good place to finish at the end of our journey together.

So, let me close this book in the same way I opened it, reflecting on a quote from Antoine de Saint-Exupéry that you will find at the top of these concluding thoughts. As I close this journey through the maze that is 'leadershift', I can't help but think that the ultimate leadership challenge is not the erosion of the powers and tools thrust upon us by a turbulent environment. The ultimate challenge for any of us is our ability to take Saint-Exupéry's first step. We cannot second-guess the future. There is no point looking for a truth that will answer all our concerns. It is not out there. Our job as leaders is to take the first step, without trying to second-guess or fearing what might lie ahead. Our future lies in our ability to march proudly into our future – at some times leaders and at others followers – working together, building on each others' strengths. With that in mind I wish you a fruitful journey and thank you for allowing me to take up some of your precious time.

Don't take my word for it

There are so many books I would like to recommend I would have to write a book of books and that would, let's be honest, not be that interesting! There are so many books I consulted as part of my research that a full bibliography would also be too huge. Instead I have decided to give you some key books that will help you get deeper into the ideas. I hope you find them as interesting as I did.

To get deeper into the trends and explore some of the more interesting facets of our potential futures here are the five books I recommend. They are great entry points into further research for those in search of answers or a powerful take on the trends for those in search of a second opinion.

Information Anxiety 2, Richard S Wurman, Que, Indiana 2001
Written by the man who created the influential Technology Enter-tainment and Design conference (www.TED.com) – which you need to check out if you have not come across it – and certainly one of the foremost trends thinkers of our age. This is a must-read.

Generation Me – Why Today's Young Americans Are More Confident, Assertive, Entitled and More Miserable Than Ever Before, Jean M Twenge, PhD, Free Press, New York 2006
To my mind, the best investigation into the generation Y phenomena and on its implications for us all. Jean Twenge has done one of the most thorough pieces of longitudinal research ever conducted in this field. She also writes brilliantly.

We Are Smarter Than Me – How to Unleash The Power Of Crowds In Your Business, B Libert and J Spector, Wharton School Publishing, New Jersey 2008
Written by a cast of thousands of contributors this book is rightly described as 'the only hands-on guide to profiting from business communities and social networking'. Read this book and marvel at what the results of the expertise trend can be.

Exodus To The Virtual World – How Online Fun is Changing Reality, Edward Castronova, Palgrave MacMillan, New York 2007
By the author of the seminal book *Synthetic World*, this new volume is a good place to start to investigate the implications of the attention trend with one of the best guides in the field by your side.

Free Agent Nation – The Future of Working For Yourself', Daniel H Pink, Warner Books, New York 2002
Still the most thorough exploration on the forces behind the democratic trend by one of the most innovative and gifted business writers of our time. Dan Pink has captured not only the data but the energy behind a relentless movement.

Below are the books that I recommend you start with if you are trying to understand more about the implications of our trends. The first is in fact three books as it contains three volumes covering different ground. However, as the old book clubs, who used to advertise their special offers on the pages of Sunday newspaper supplements (remember them), would have said, the three volumes count as one choice!

The Information Age – Economy, Society and Culture, Manuel Castells, Blackwell Publishers, 1996

Don't be fooled by the date of publication, Manuel Castells' words are still as relevant and up to date as when they were first published. In three volumes he charts the course of society and organizations through the three trends pointing out critical implications along the way.

I, Avatar – The Culture and Consequences of Having a Second Life, Mark Stephen Meadows, New Riders, Berkeley, CA 2008
This book is as close to an anthropological study of SL as you're going to get. The advantage is that it is written with great charm and humour rather than dry scholarly language.

Wikinomics – How Mass Collaboration Changes Everything, Don Tapscott, Anthony Williams, Portfolio, 2006
Arguably the first book to have brought together a number of vast disparate themes and built a coherent picture of the 'so what' of mass collaboration.

Community – The Structure of Belonging, Peter Block, Berrett-Koehler Publishers, 2008
Peter Block turns his attention to what makes a community work and what we can do to transform the places we care about.

Netocracy – The New Power Elite And Life After Capitalism, Alexander Bard, Jan Soderqvist, Pearson Education Limited, 2002
This is a wonderful map of the post-trends environment and the actors shaping it.

These following titles do not represent a complete overview of the field of networked or distributed leadership. However, each offers a broader perspective than most 'how to' books which are still rooted in a very simplistic form of the organization and the nature and source of a leader's power.

Tribes – We need you to lead us, Seth Godin, Portfolio, 2008
If you ever think that new organizational forms do not require leaders this is your book. If you think they do but are not sure what a leader looks like in these tribes then this is your book too. In summary, just read it!

Understanding Institutional Diversity, Elinor Ostrom, Princeton University Press, 2005
This book charts the make-up of institutions (open and closed) as well as their norms and rules of governance to help us understand how communities form and behave.

Followership – How Followers are Creating Change and Changing Leaders, Barbara Kellerman, Harvard Business Press, 2008
Starting from the very prescient insight that much more has been written about leaders than their followers, Barbara Kellerman helps us understand the needs and wants of followers.

Once You're Lucky, Twice You're Good – The Rebirth of Silicon Valley And The Rise of Web 2.0, Sarah Lacy, Gotham Books, 2008
This is a book about the people who are shaping social communities in web 2.0 and are being shaped by them.

The Hidden Connections, Fritjof Capra, Flamingo, 2003
Although not a leadership title per se, *The Hidden Connections* is an in-depth analysis of what systems look like and the role of agents within them.

A Crowd of One – The Future Of Individual Identity, John Henry Clippinger, PublicAffairs, 2007
A look at how our desires for communal relationships rather than needs for individualistic pursuits are shaping our identity.

Not surprisingly, the subjects of complexity and clarity are hot topics in business today. The advent of complexity theory a few years ago has meant that bookshelves are now full of titles that promise to make life easier (or at least help you cope with it better). I have chosen the five books that I reckon should give you as wide an overview as possible of the whole area.

The Laws of Simplicity – Design, Technology, Business, Life, John Maeda, The MIT Press, 2006

This indispensable little book tackles the issue of coherence, providing invaluable lessons for business along the way.

Thoughts – Creating Value By Design, Stefano Marzano, Lund Humphries Publishers, 1998
Stefano Marzano (Director of the Philips Design Group), offers us powerful insights on the biggest problem we are grappling with as a generation – making sense of our world.

Reassembling the Social – An Introduction to Actor-Network-Theory, Bruno Latour, Oxford University Press, 2005
Fellow Burgundian Latour provides the clearest introduction to the complex but critical topic of actor-network-theory.

Herd – How To Change Mass Behaviour By Harnessing Our True Nature, Mark Earls, John Wiley & Sons, 2007
Earls shows how our behaviours are rooted in social interactions and draws lessons for business leaders.

The Social Atom – Why The Rich Get Richer, Cheats Get Caught And Your Neighbor Usually Looks Like You, Mark Buchanan, Cyan, 2007
This book is for all of us who have struggled to understand some of the finer mathematical insights of Nobel Prize winner Thomas Schelling. The big lesson is you will only find coherence if you 'look at patterns not at people'.

Storytelling seems to be all the rage so many books have been written about it and most are somewhere on the bestseller shelves of your local bookstore. I am worried however that a lot of what is written is more about how to create a convincing story to encourage people rather than about the role narratives can play in creating real adaptive communities. I therefore like to look outside the business genre for deeper insights into the power of narratives.

The Seven Basic Plots – Why We Tell Stories, Christopher Booker, Continuum, 2004

With over 700 pages, this is not a book for the faint-hearted, but a book that took 34 years to write deserves at least 34 of your precious hours to be read. It explores how stories emerge and looks at the human condition's need for them.

Making Comics – Storytelling Secrets of Comics, Manga and Graphic Novels, Scott McCloud, Harper, 2006
For business readers this is an important work as it explains how emotions can be called upon and attention sustained through a visual narrative.

The Hero With A Thousand Faces, Joseph Campbell, Fontana Press, 1993
This book is a classic. In it Joseph Campbell explores myths to draw the essence of the hero's journey.

Story – Substance, Structure, Style, And The Principles of Screenwriting, Robert McKee, Methuen, 1999
The Hollywood writing coach helps us understand how narratives move a plot forward and create coherence for anyone watching a film.

Presentation Zen – Simple Ideas on Presentation Design and Delivery, Garr Reynolds, Continuum, 2004
This wonderful volume focuses on the fundamental of narratives – your impact (for more visit Garr's excellent blog www.presentationzen.com).

To understand the consequences of the DEAD trends for the way we think about work (in particular our relationship with roles and tasks), we must draw from a wide variety of sources (psychological, sociological, philosophical and political). The five titles I have chosen to illustrate, inform and reinforce the points I have made in this chapter all fall into one or more of these categories.

The Corrosion of Character – The Personal Consequences Of Work In The New Capitalism, Richard Sennett, W W Norton & Company, 1999

In this seminal book Sennett looks at the world of work through a sociological, philosophical and political lens to draw lessons on what this might mean for the way we progress in our search for meaning.

Culture Shift – In Advanced Industrial Society, Ronald Inglehart, Princeton University Press, 1990
This monumental work examines how economic, sociological and technological trends are impacting our culture and the way we work.

ID – The Quest for Identity In The 21st Century, Susan Greenfield, Sceptre, 2008
This book explores how we shape our identity given the technological changes we are witnessing and what this means for communities.

Social Role Valorization: The English Experience, David G Race, Whiting & Birch Ltd, 2006
Social Role Valorization provides food for thought on the development of self-image and social role and the accountabilities this creates.

Role Motivation Theories, John B Miner, Routledge, 1993
Understanding the type of motivation that underpins a communal effort is critical to understanding the nature of accountabilities.

There is a huge library of books on motivation, reward, recognition and incentives available with most titles offering insights on the areas discussed in our 'love chapter'. I have chosen the five books which, for different reasons, I think best illustrate what I have been writing about here.

Love Is The Killer App – How to Win Business And Influence Friends, Tim Sanders, Random House Inc, 2002
I recommend this book to anyone looking to make an impact in their organization. Read it please.

Love, Leo Buscaglia, Souvenir Press, 1972
This book emerged from the discussions Buscaglia and his students had on what love is, what it could be, how it could be developed and why it matters.

Creating Commitment – How To Attract And Retain Talented Employees By Building Relationships That Last, Michael N O'Malley, John Wiley & Sons, Inc., 2000
The author looks at how commitment comes about and how it can be maintained. He covers a wide field of research leading him to make valuable and informative observations.

Predictably Irrational – The Hidden Forces That Shape Our Decisions, Dan Ariely, Harper Collins Publishers, 2008
Economic and incentive-based models are predicated on the idea that human beings are, in the main, rational. Ariely, a behavioral economist, takes issue with that idea and tests it to destruction.

Stumbling On Happiness – Why The Future Won't Feel The Way You Think It Will..., Daniel Gilbert, Harper Collins Publishers, 2006
Covering a wide and varied field and using some of the latest findings on how our brain works, Professor Gilbert shows us how we make decisions on our future and how poor those are.

Communities form, grow and dissolve in line with the nature and strength of the conversations their members generate. Strong social and cultural ties help adaptation and change. If we want to once and for all get rid of the 'Elvis Fallacy' we're going to understand the practical value of conversations. Titles in this field span many disciplines and schools of thought. I have chosen the five books below because they provide a balance between thoughts and practice. Reading these should help you perceive the Elvis fallacy for what it is – a short road to failure to engage.

Conversations – How Talk Can Change Your Life, Theodore Zeldin, The Harvill Press, 1998
In an age where dialogue and conversations are still seen as the preserve of the loud and 'charismatic', where the skilful is seen as more productive than the thoughtful, Zeldin takes us on a tour of what conversations mean and deliver.

Made To Stick – Why Some Ideas Take Hold And Others Come Unstuck, Chip and Dan Heath, Random House Books, 2007
By laying out the elements of 'stickiness' (simple, unexpected, concrete, credible, emotional, stories – SUCCESs) and providing examples that meet all of them, the Heath brothers illustrate the power of conversations.

Dialogue – And The Art Of Thinking Together, William Isaacs, Doubleday, 1999
This is as complete a volume on the power of dialogue in moving businesses forward as you are likely to find. It offers practical advice underpinned by useful models.

Fierce Conversations – Achieving Success In Work And In Life, One Conversation At A Time, Susan Scott, Piatkus, 2002
By offering seven principles that distil the essence of conversational skills, Scott moves away from our obsession with communication skills to focus on our conversational abilities.

The World Café – Shaping Our Future Through Conversations That Matter, Juanita Brown and David Isaacs, Berrett-Koehler Publishers, Inc, 2005
This book offers a practical toolkit for anyone wishing to stage new conversations in organizations.

The books in this list are all available somewhere either first- or second-hand. Some may need a bit more searching than others but I hope you find the search rewarding and if you have any more suggestions, do let me know.

Index

NB: page numbers in *italic* indicate figures or tables

ALSO AVAILABLE FROM KOGAN PAGE

ISBN: 978 0 7494 5276 6 Paperback 2008

PRAISE FOR *THE CONNECTED LEADER*

"Occasionally a management book is published which triggers a paradigm shift in business philosophy. The Connected Leader *is such a book. Emmanuel Gobillot has written the first leadership book for the MySpace generation."*

Claire Mason, CEO, Man Bites Dog

"We are at our best when we feel a part of something meaningful and important. Emmanuel Gobillot goes beyond helping us to envision effective leaders to creating the power of possibilities with engaged leaders. He integrates observations from a huge number of fields and industries to bring a fantastic exploration of the essence of great leadership relationships – being connected and engaged!"

Professor Richard Boyatzis, Departments of Psychology and Organizational Behaviour, Case Western Reserve University, Adjunct Professor of Human Resources, ESADE, co-author of *Resonant Leadership* and the international best-seller *Primal Leadership*

"The book deserves a place in every manager's bookcase."

Training Journal

"Reading The Connected Leader *you feel as if Gobillot has invited you to join his informal network, to be one of his special contacts, and that you have been given a privileged insight into understanding through his vast array of assessment tools your own organization, and how informal networks can be used to make change happen."*

Michael Millward MSc for the CIP North Yorkshire Newsletter